NYLEGS

Photographs by Stacey Baker © 2016
Introduction by Kathy Ryan
Design by Matt Willey
Copy editing by Harvey Dickson
Image processing by Ethan Jones
Production by Kehrer Design Heidelberg (Andreas Schubert)

First Edition
Printed and bound in Germany
ISBN 978-3-86828-698-4

Kehrer Heidelberg Berlin
www.kehrerverlag.com

NY LEGS

By
Stacey
Baker

Introduction by Kathy Ryan

When Stacey Baker spots a good pair of legs, she has to move quickly. Sometimes she races down the sidewalk to catch the woman before she slips out of sight. Sometimes she sidles up and gently introduces herself. Quickly, she persuades the stranger to pose for her by whipping her iPhone out of her pocket, showing some of the images on her stace-a-lace Instagram account and explaining that she needs the woman to stand up against a particular wall and raise her arms above her head. Baker does not allow any hands or arms in her pictures. She always frames them so the subject is cut off at the waist. She asks her muse to stand in front of a gritty, textured wall and composes each image so that the heels line up with the horizon line, where the wall meets the sidewalk. By following this disciplined approach, Baker has figured out a way to commandeer a portrait studio out of the chaos of Midtown Manhattan.

A handful were made elsewhere, but all the photographs in this book were taken in New York City. Of these, about a third are made on one block of 40th Street, between 7th and 8th Avenues. This block was chosen for practical as much as artistic reasons. Baker makes many of these pictures on her lunch hour, and this is the block where she works as a photo editor at The New York Times Magazine. The block is rich in women sporting wild legwear. Baker has found women wearing leggings printed with cats' faces, peacock feathers, Batman logos, long-stemmed roses, Hokusai's wave, hearts, crosses, trees, eyeballs, crests, castles, stars, lips, eyelashes, fingernails and the word "love" repeated over and over. There are lots of eye-popping black-and-white geometric patterns such as zigzags, stripes and triangles, as well as animal prints and rainbows of color. What the leggings all have in common is that they are skintight. Body-hugging jeans have clearly also been a theme of the portfolio, particularly if they are shredded, cut-up or bleached in unexpected ways, with flesh showing through the holes. Shorts worn over tights or fishnet stockings is another popular look. There are demure looks, too, such as a blue crocheted miniskirt worn with black tights and booties. Often miniskirts are paired with something rugged, like black ankle boots with thick soles, heavy socks pulled up above the knees or strappy gladiator sandals. One woman's long, slim legs are tightly bound from ankle to crotch with a white string and a black string. We can imagine the delight Baker felt when she spotted this one. These looks will eventually become extinct, as all fashion does. But, fortunately, we will have this extraordinary record of the era.

Baker made the first picture when she saw a woman with legs she envied at the Waldorf Astoria Hotel. She was compelled to document them. Although initially drawn to classically beautiful legs of the tall, slim variety, she eventually found herself most drawn to the fuller, fleshier versions. They have more sculptural qualities. The corporeal aspects of the women are what truly engage Baker's eye. She is more interested in the human form than in fashion. With this work, Baker has added her own brilliantly eccentric twist to the tradition of street photography. Bernd and Hilla Becher, the forerunners of the Düsseldorf School, would have recognized a like-minded soul in Stacey Baker. Her obsessive cataloguing of women's legs in rigorously composed images follows in the tradition of photographic typologies that the Bechers began with their documentation of water towers, gas refineries and coal silos in the 1950s. The genius of Baker's work lies in the way it takes this conceptual approach and reinvents it by taking it to the streets and applying it to living, breathing women.

It's no surprise that this series has been so enthusiastically received by the Instagram community. What could have been deemed an objectification or exploitation of women's bodies has been embraced as the opposite. From the comments on Baker's account, it is clear that her followers, over 78,000 now, are overwhelmingly female, and they see empowerment, pride and a strutting of personal expression in Baker's subjects. Her work has become a celebration of the diversity of female shapes.

At this point, Baker has posted over 1,000 pictures. As sometimes happens with artists – the lucky ones – she found a subject that won't let her go. It crept up on her. First she fell in love with the ease of making pictures with a cellphone. Then she fell in love with the crazy, kaleidoscopic diversity of women's legs in N.Y.C. The ease of making pictures with a cellphone has sparked a revolution in photography. Baker's body of work is among the most powerful to come out of this moment in technology, fashion and people watching other people.

Kathy Ryan is the Director of Photography at The New York Times Magazine.

10th Ave., near 23rd St.

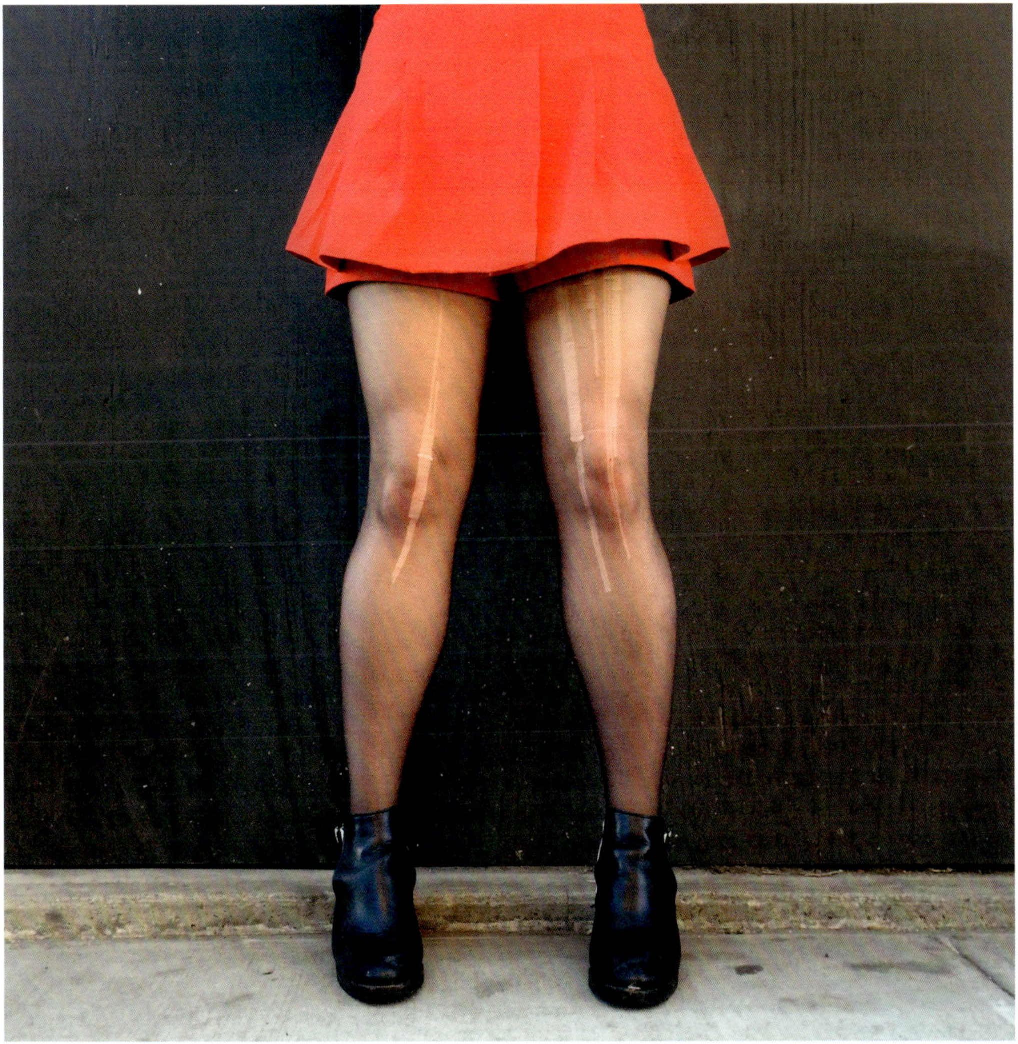

12th St., near 5th Ave.

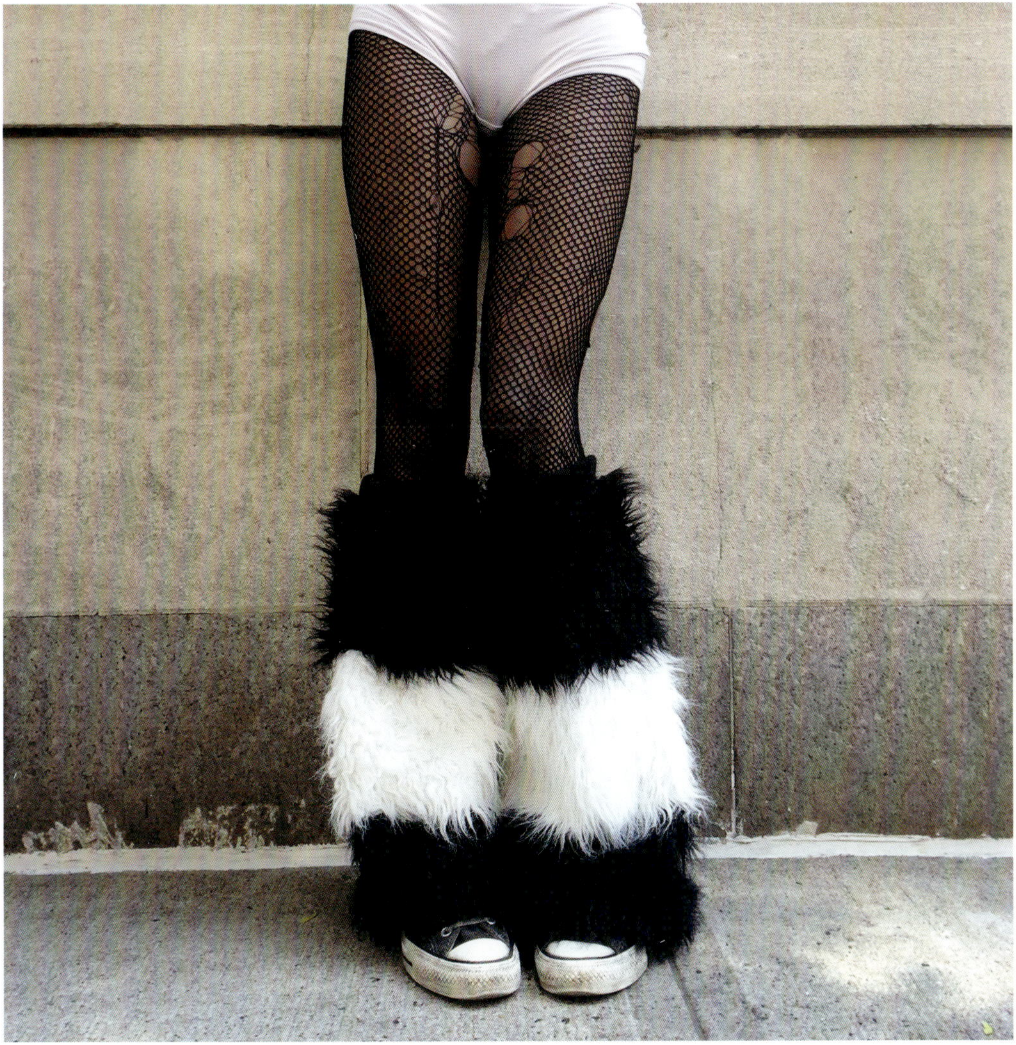

39th St., near 8th Ave.

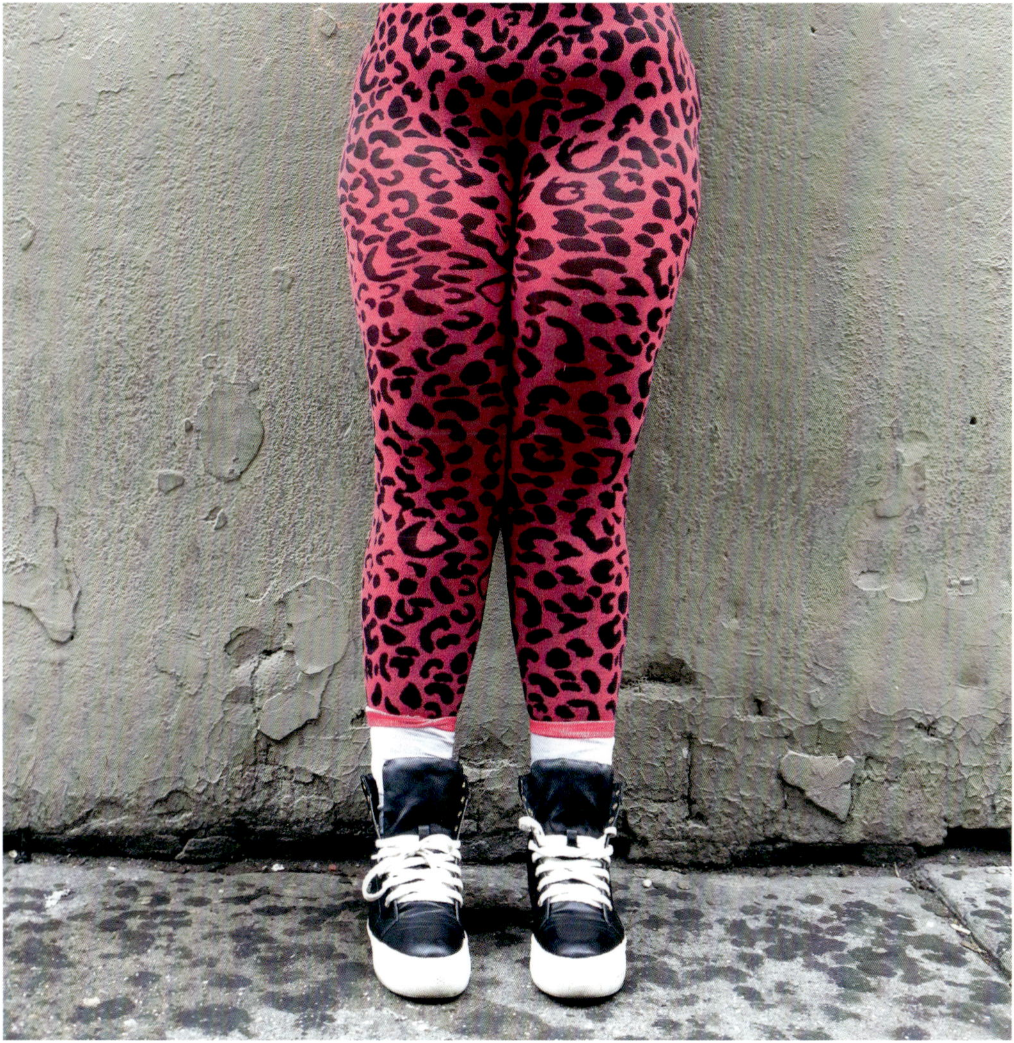

40th St., between 7th & 8th Aves.

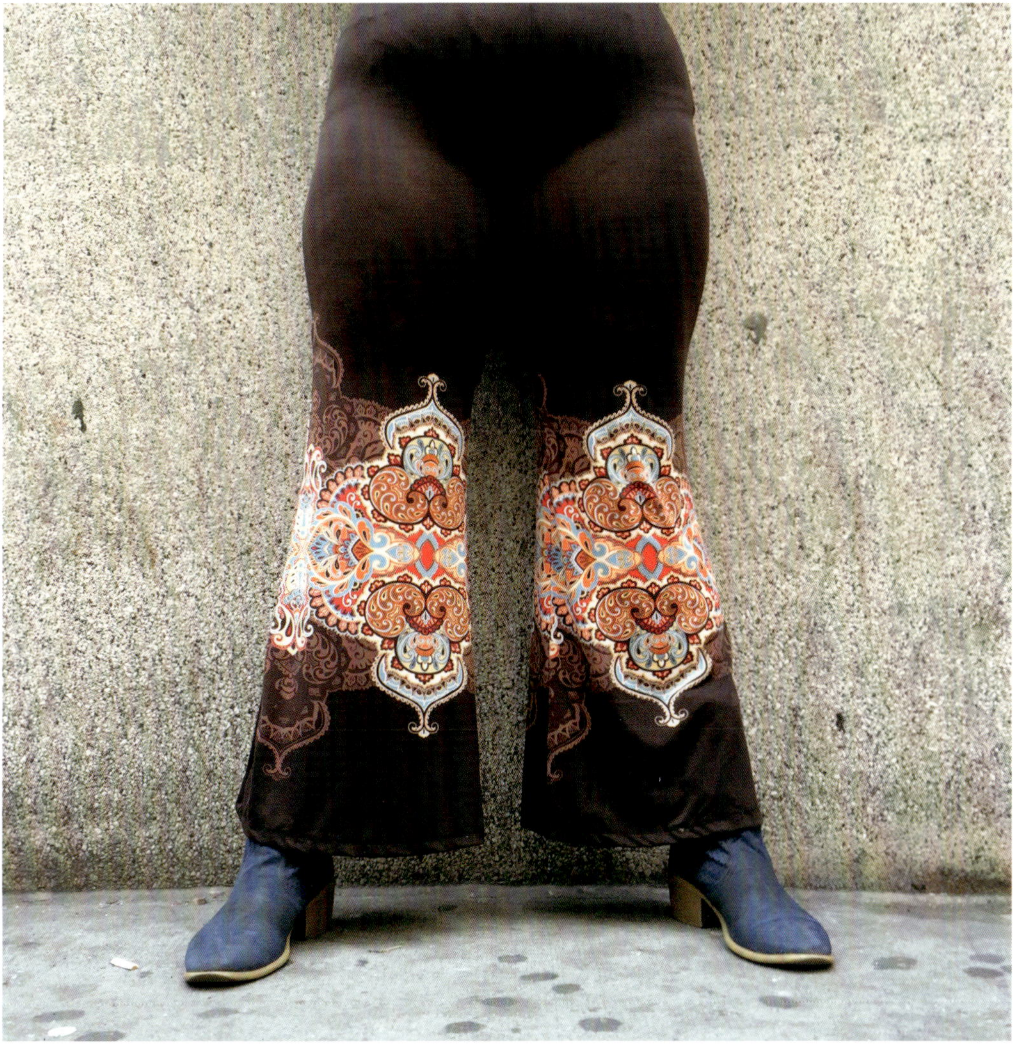

18th St. & Broadway.

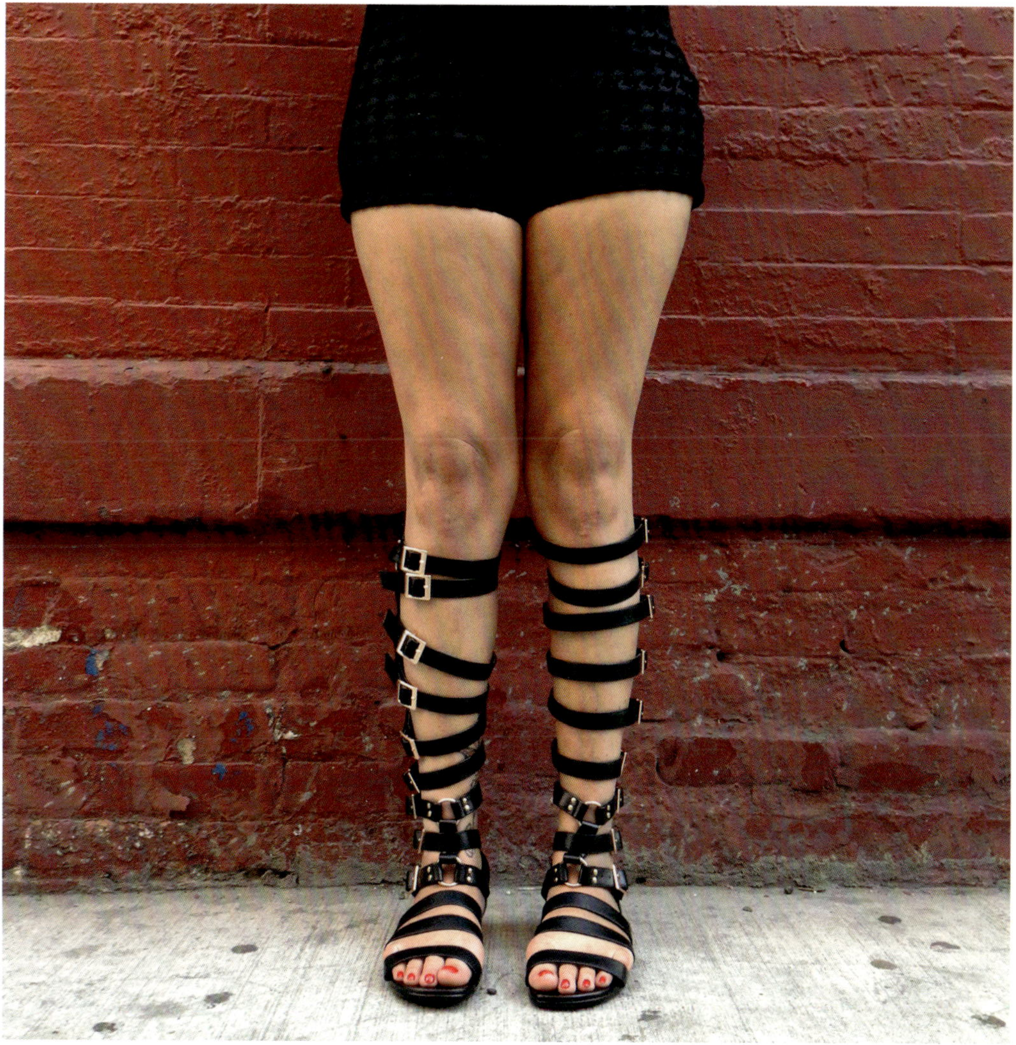

40th St., between 7th & 8th Aves.

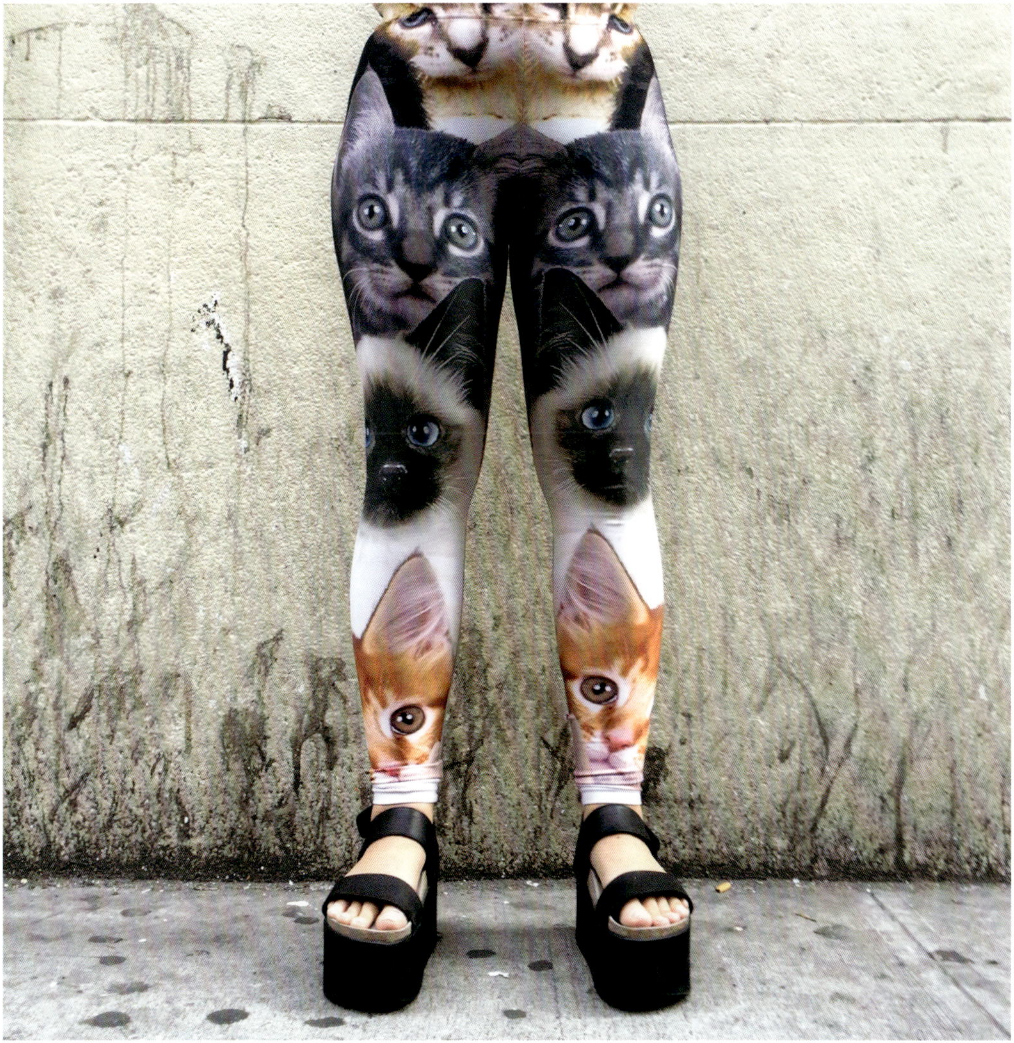

40th St., between 7th & 8th Aves.

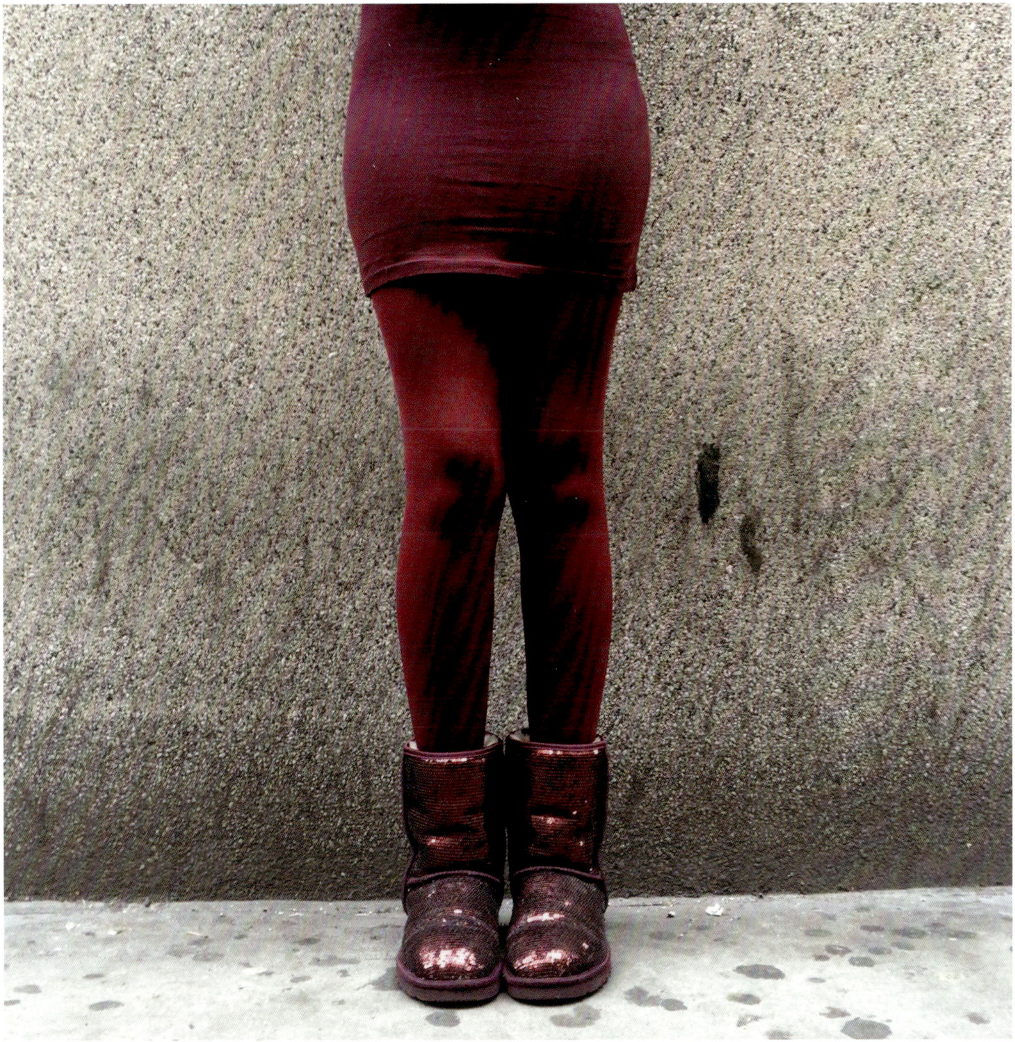

43rd St. & Lexington Ave.

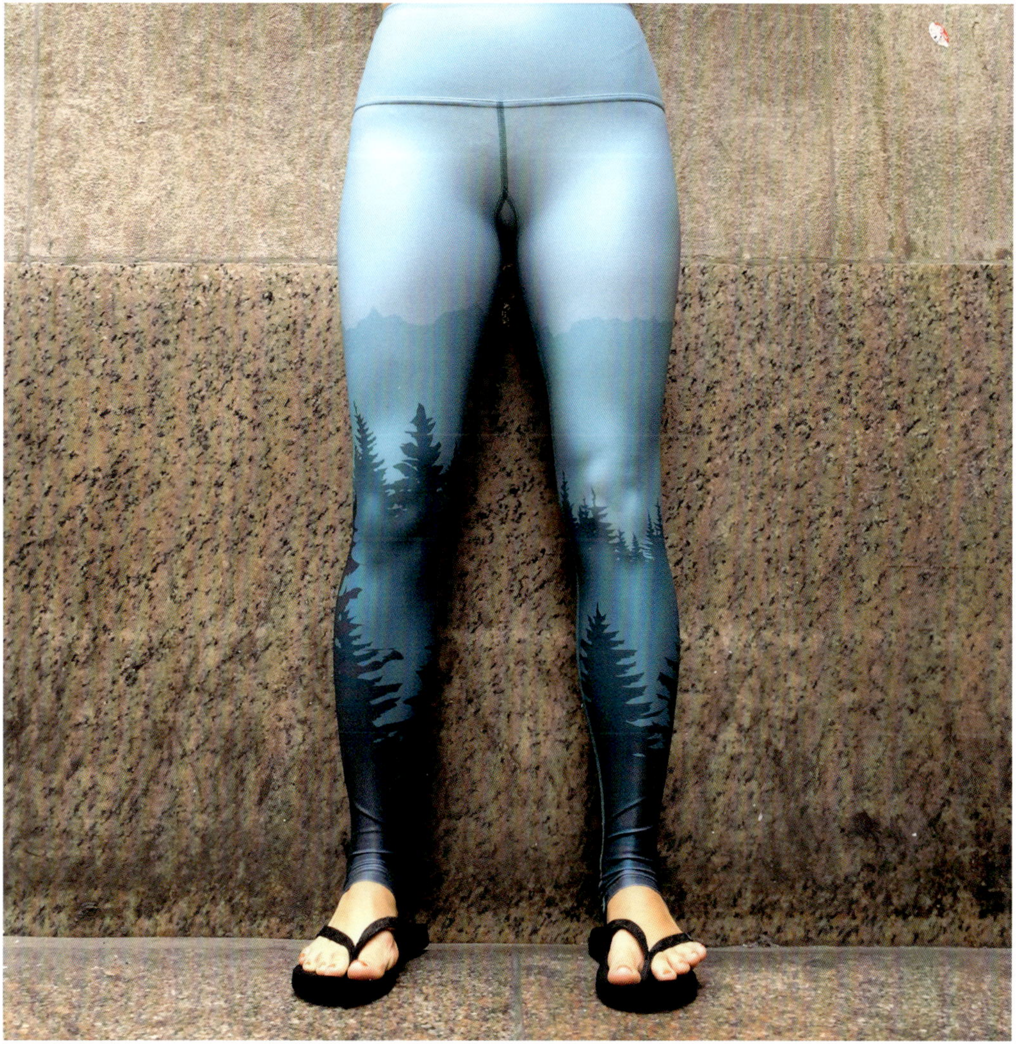

125th St., near Saint Nicholas Ave.

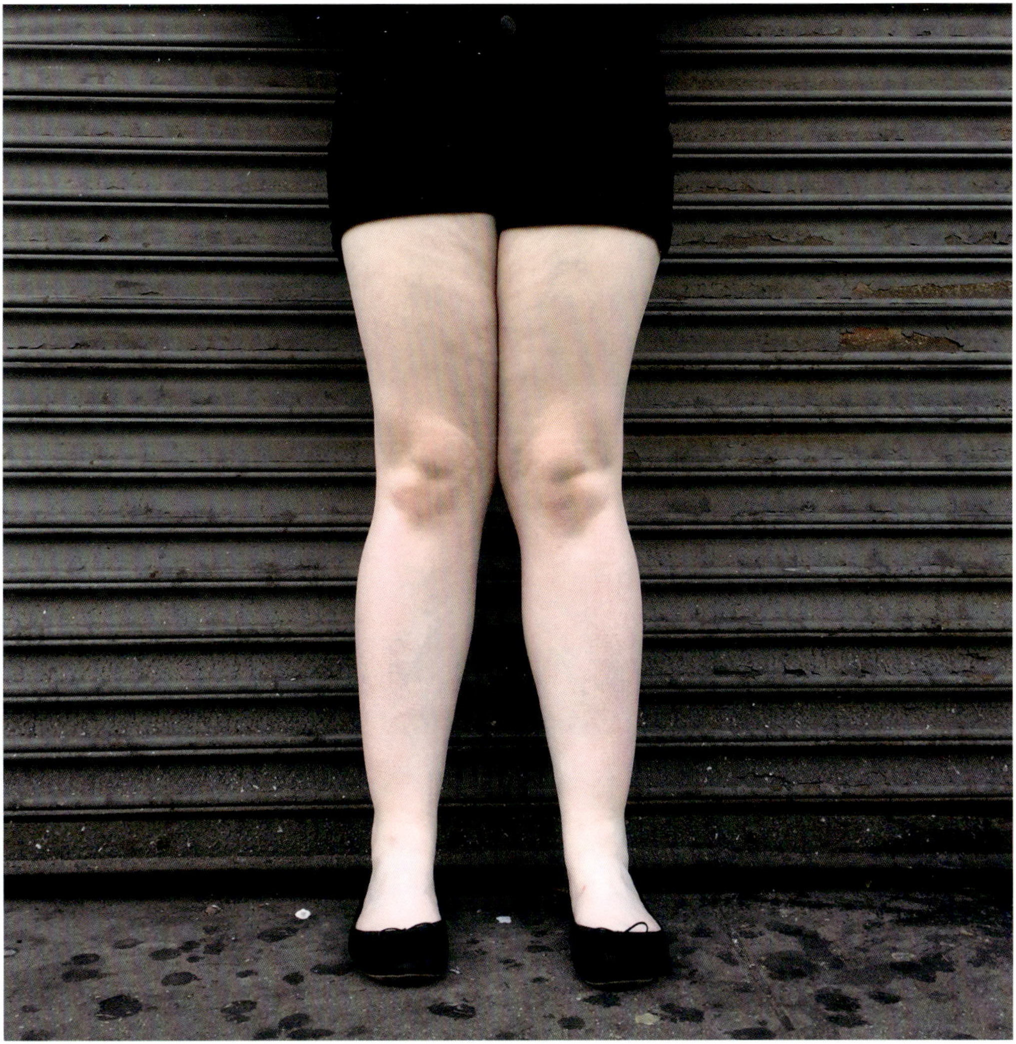

40th St., between 7th & 8th Aves.

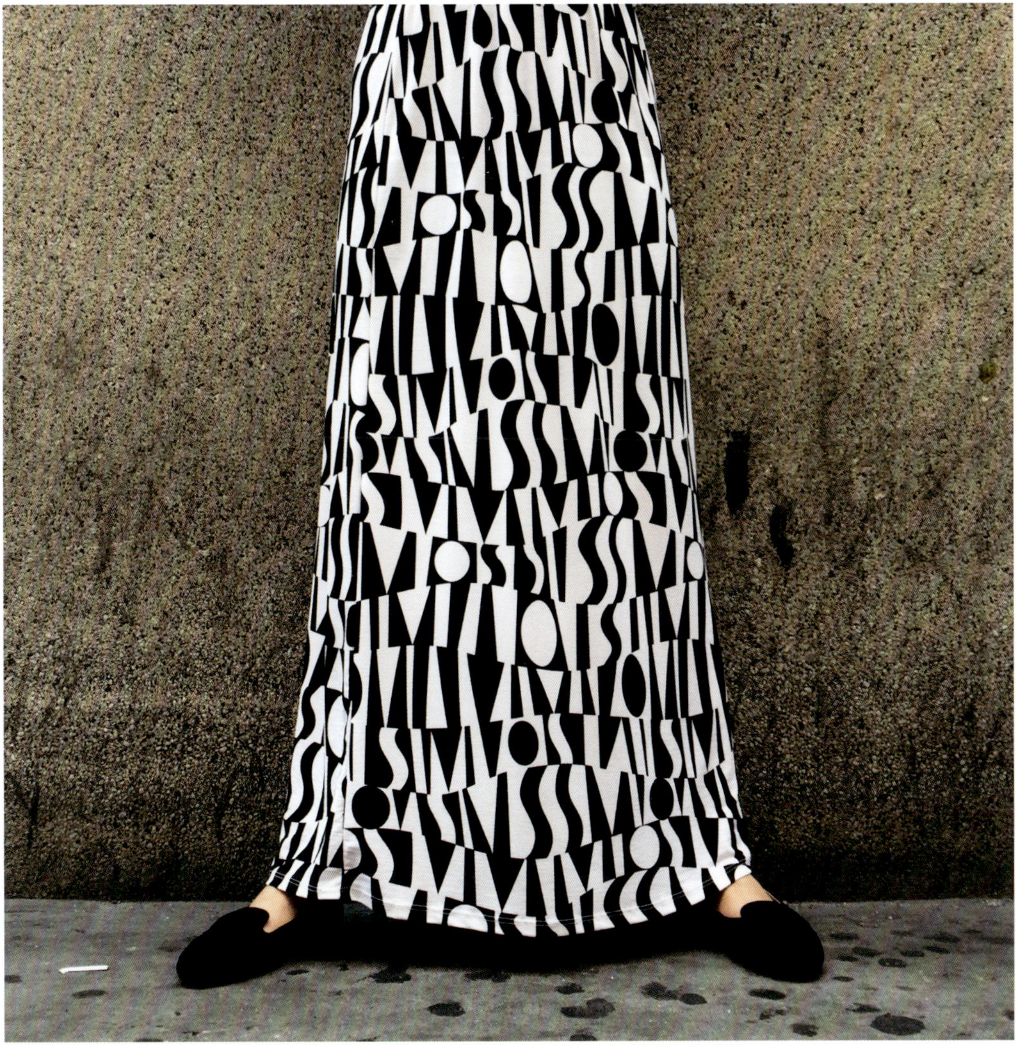

10th St., near 5th Ave.

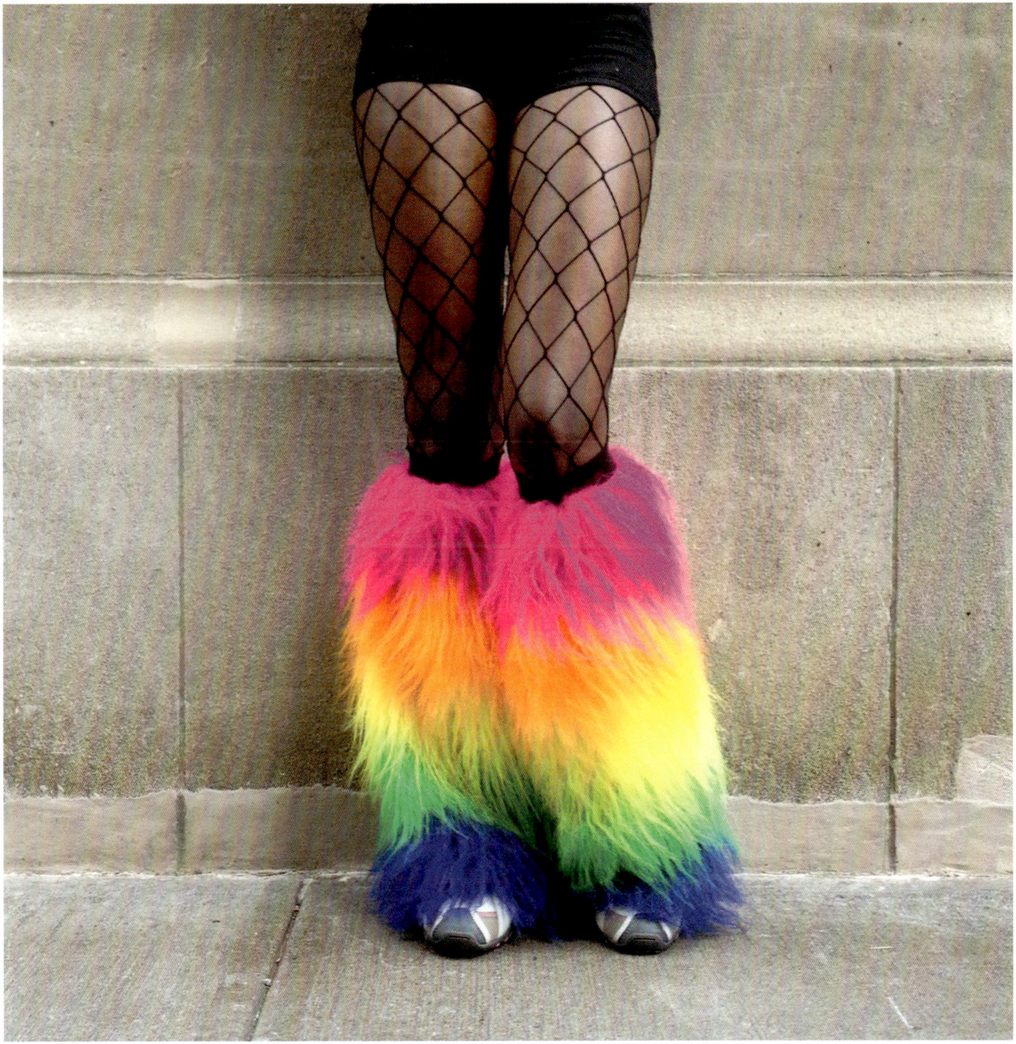

38th St. & Broadway.

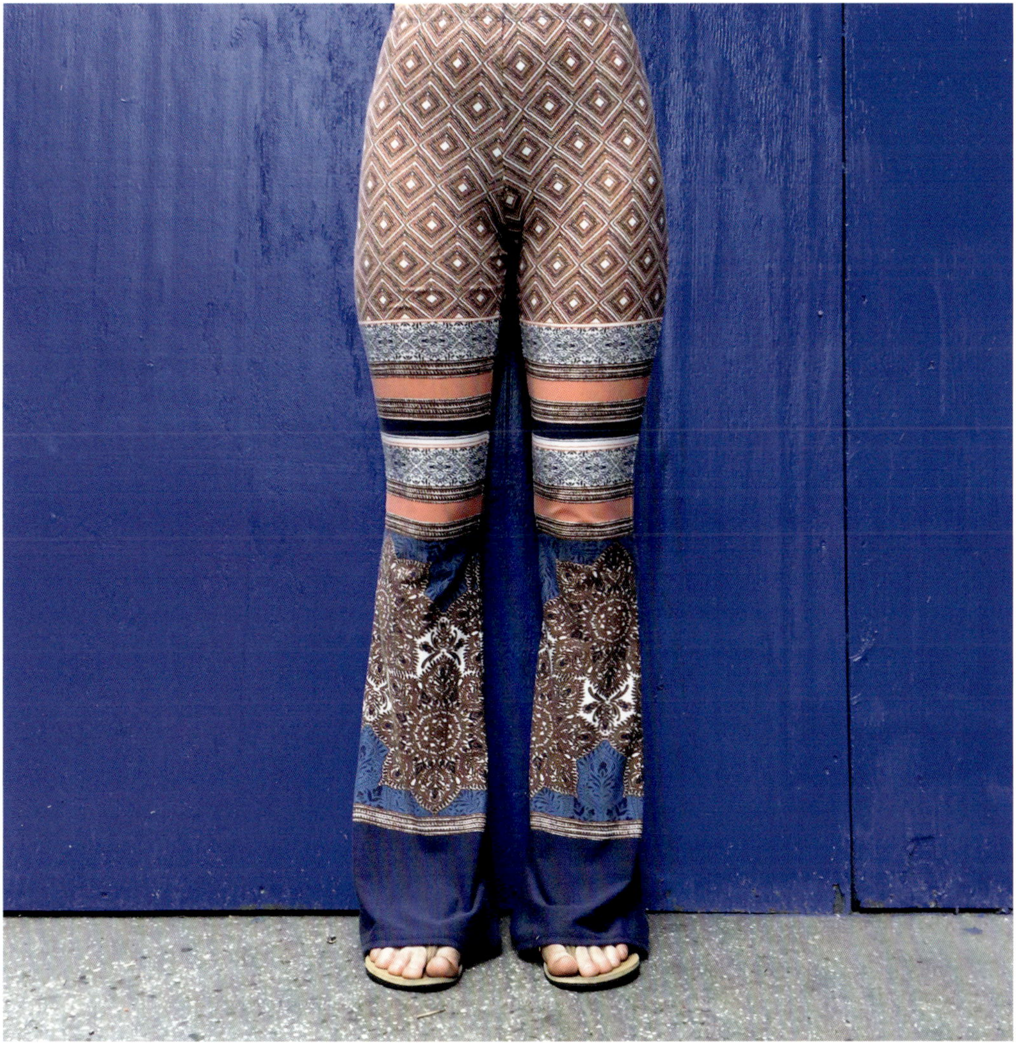

39th St., near 8th Ave.

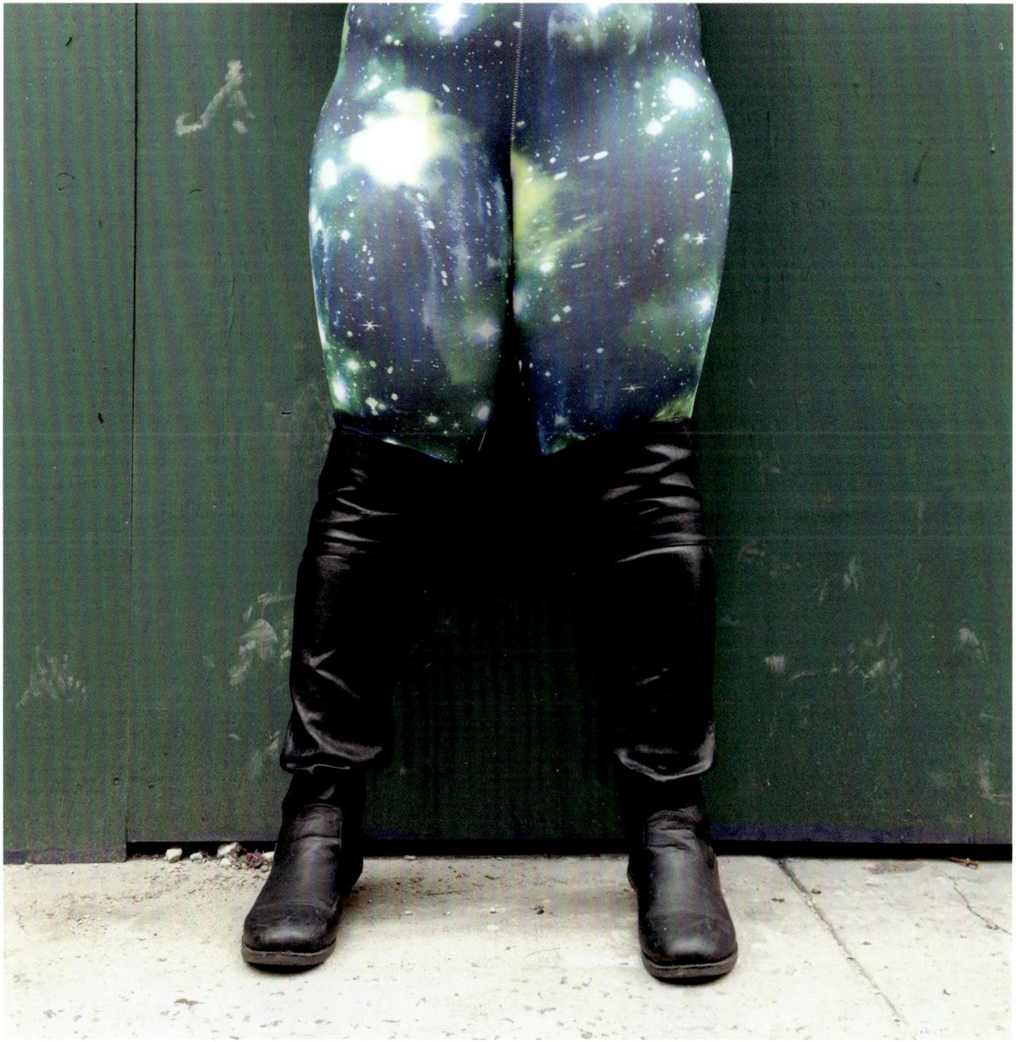

40th St., between 7th & 8th Aves.

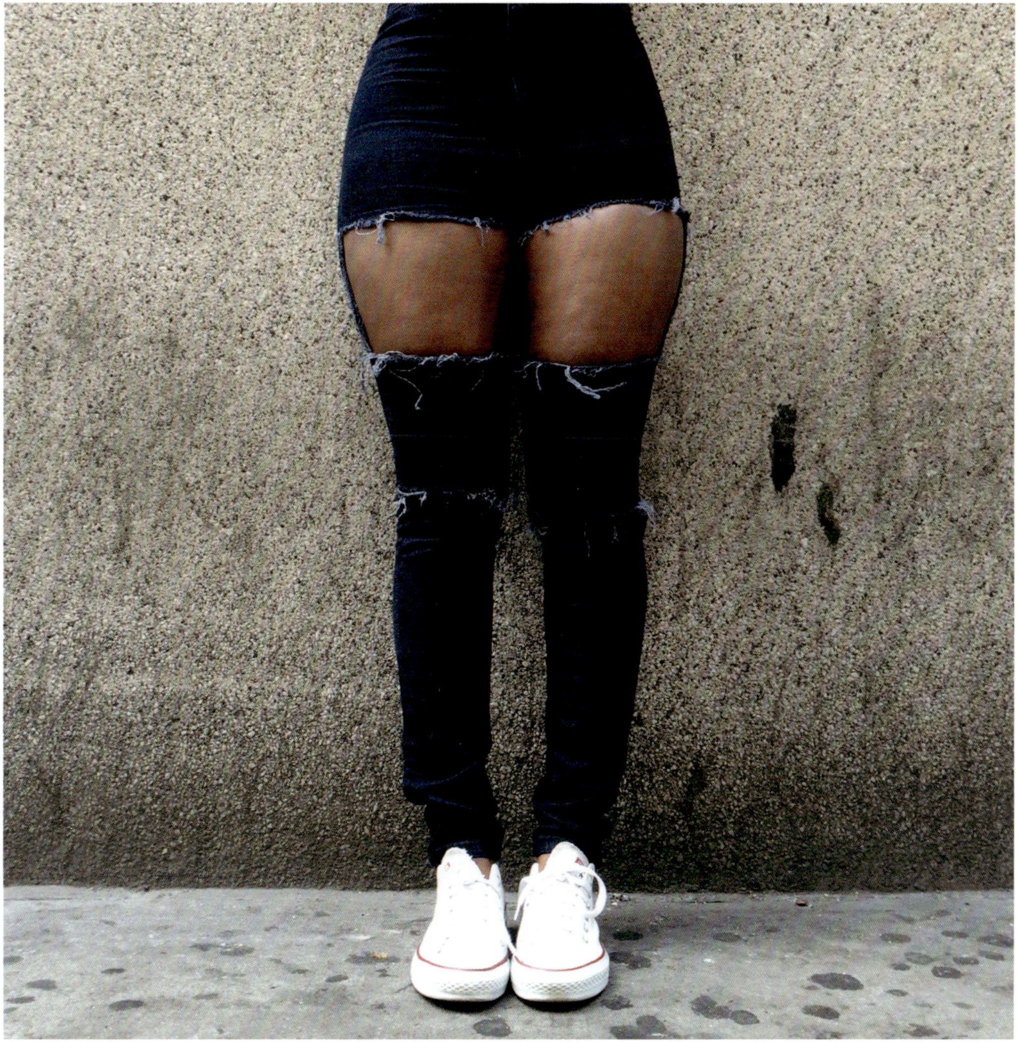

40th St., between 7th & 8th Aves.

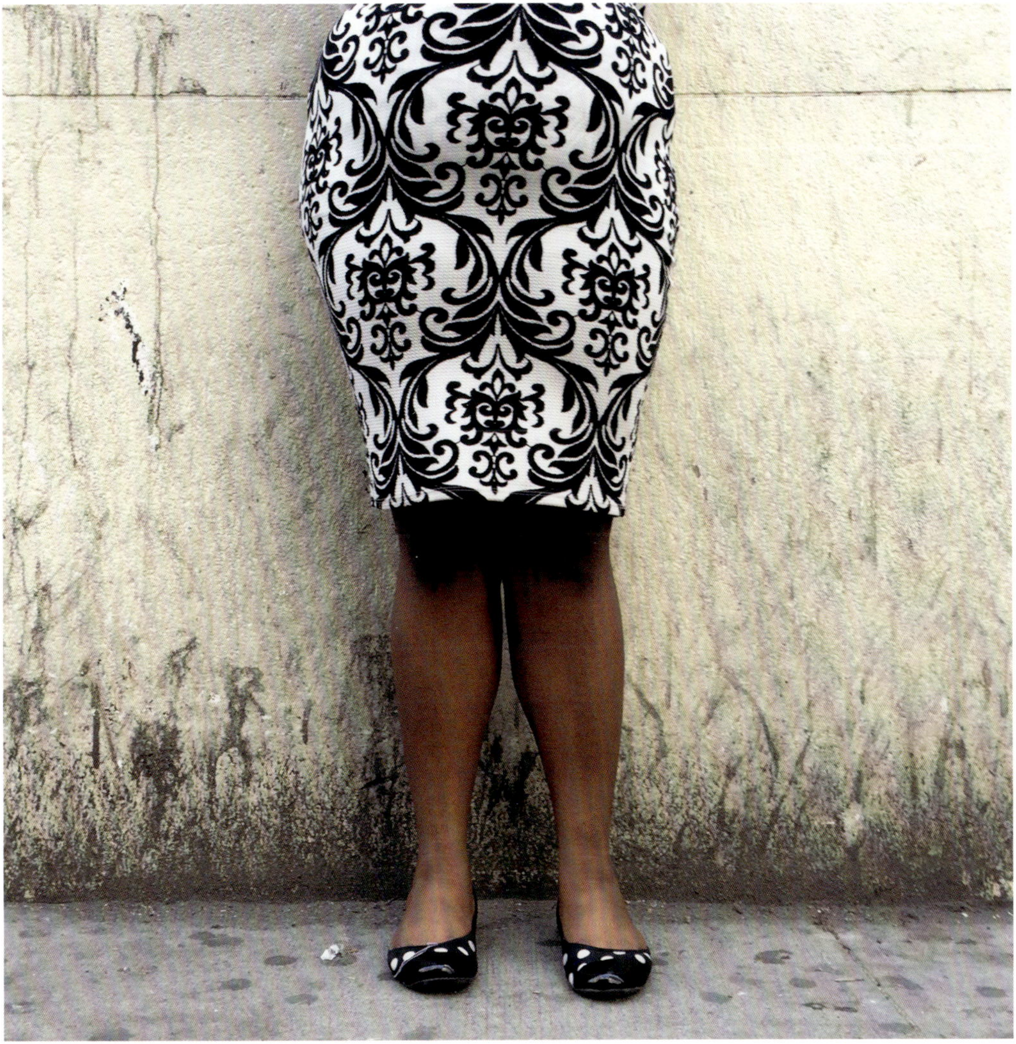

Bleecker St., near Mulberry St.

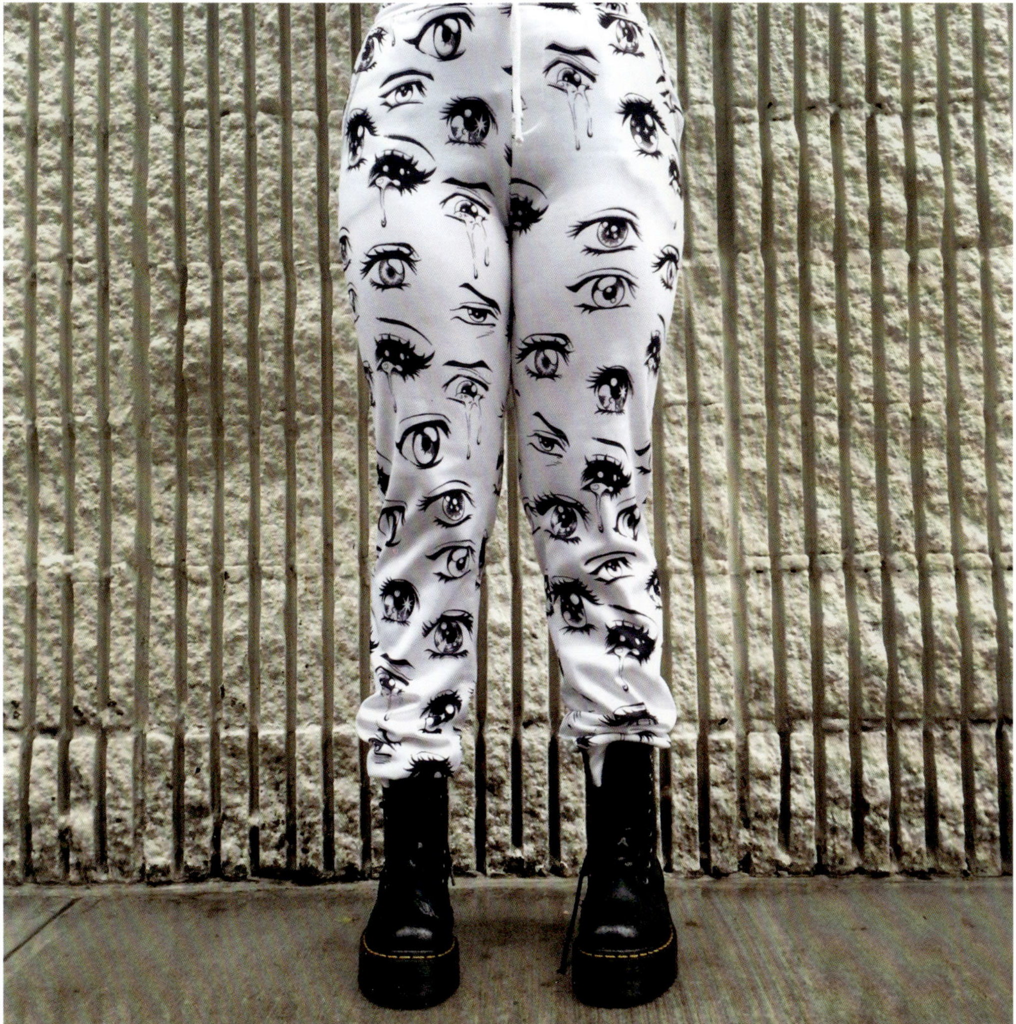

40th St., between 7th & 8th Aves.

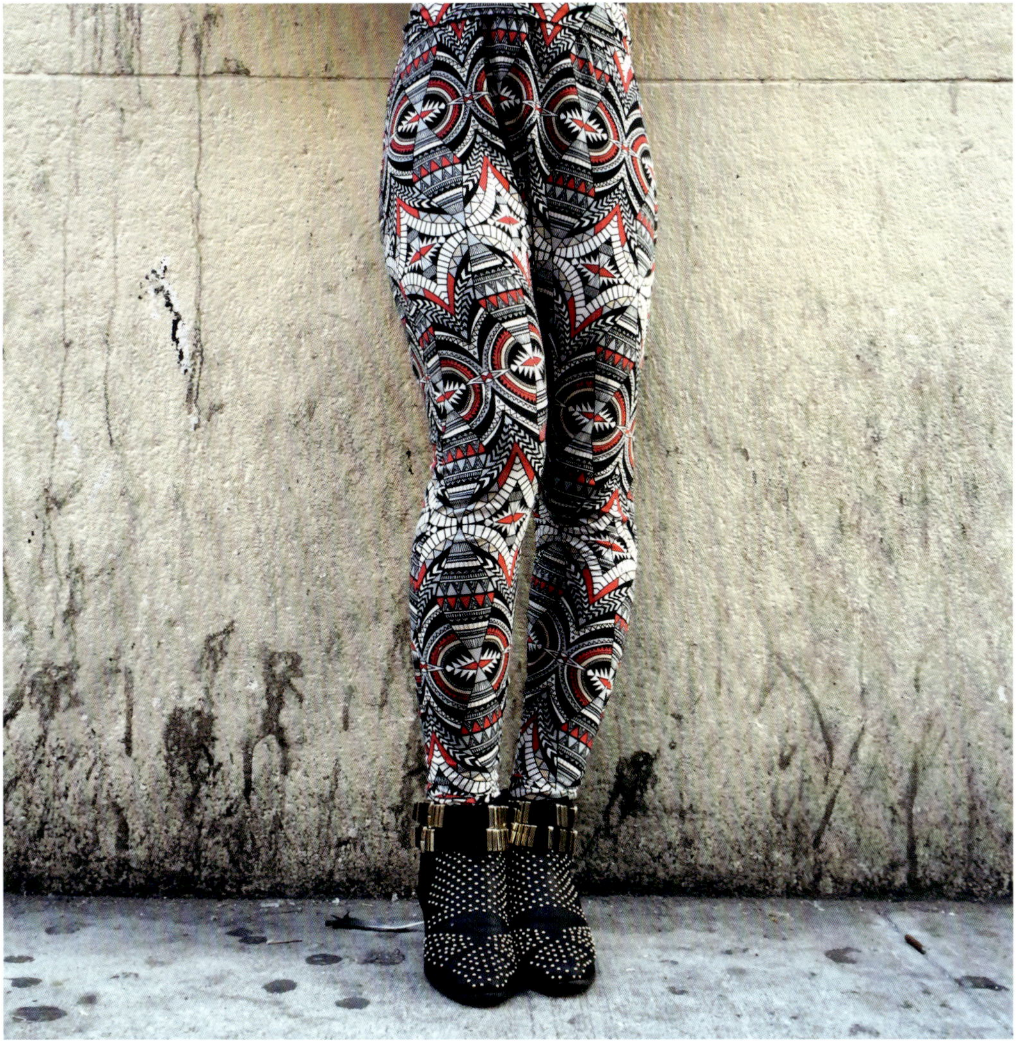

14th St., near 5th Ave.

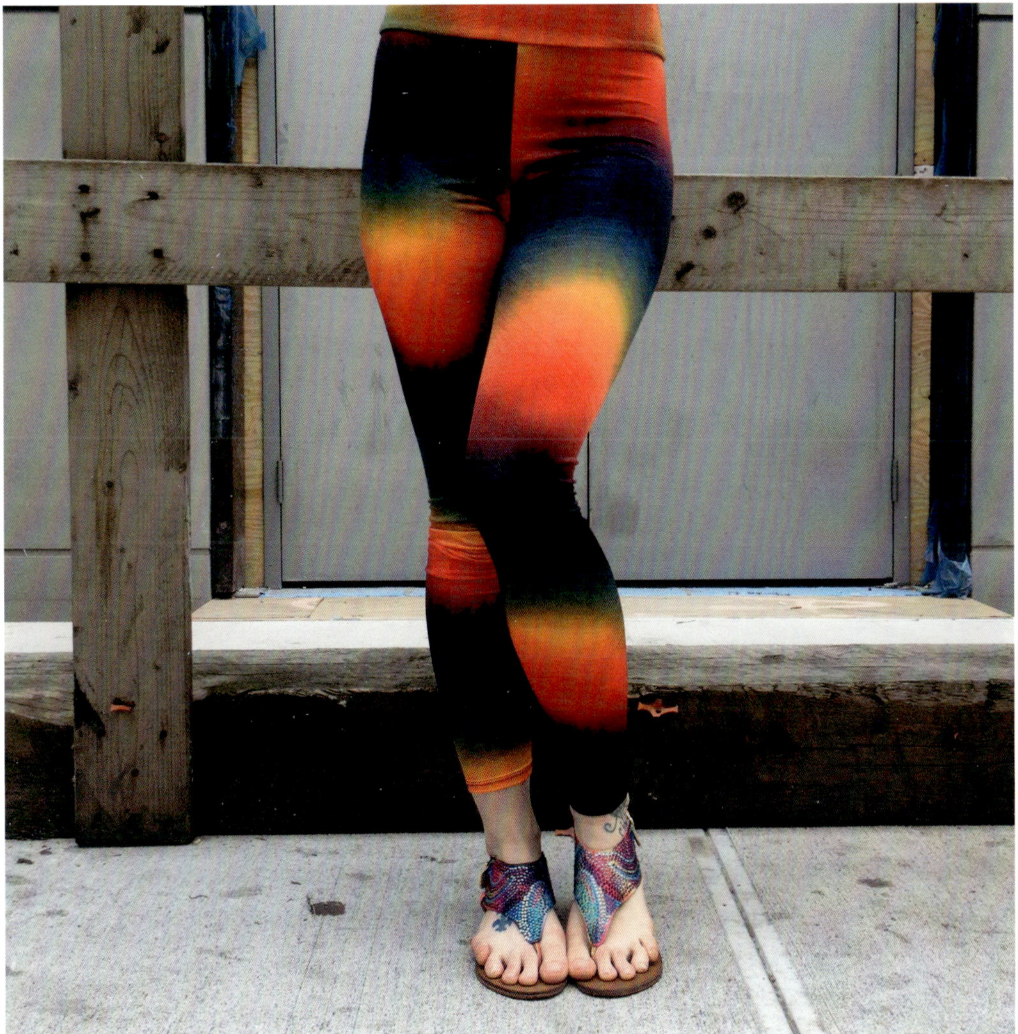

40th St., between 7th & 8th Aves.

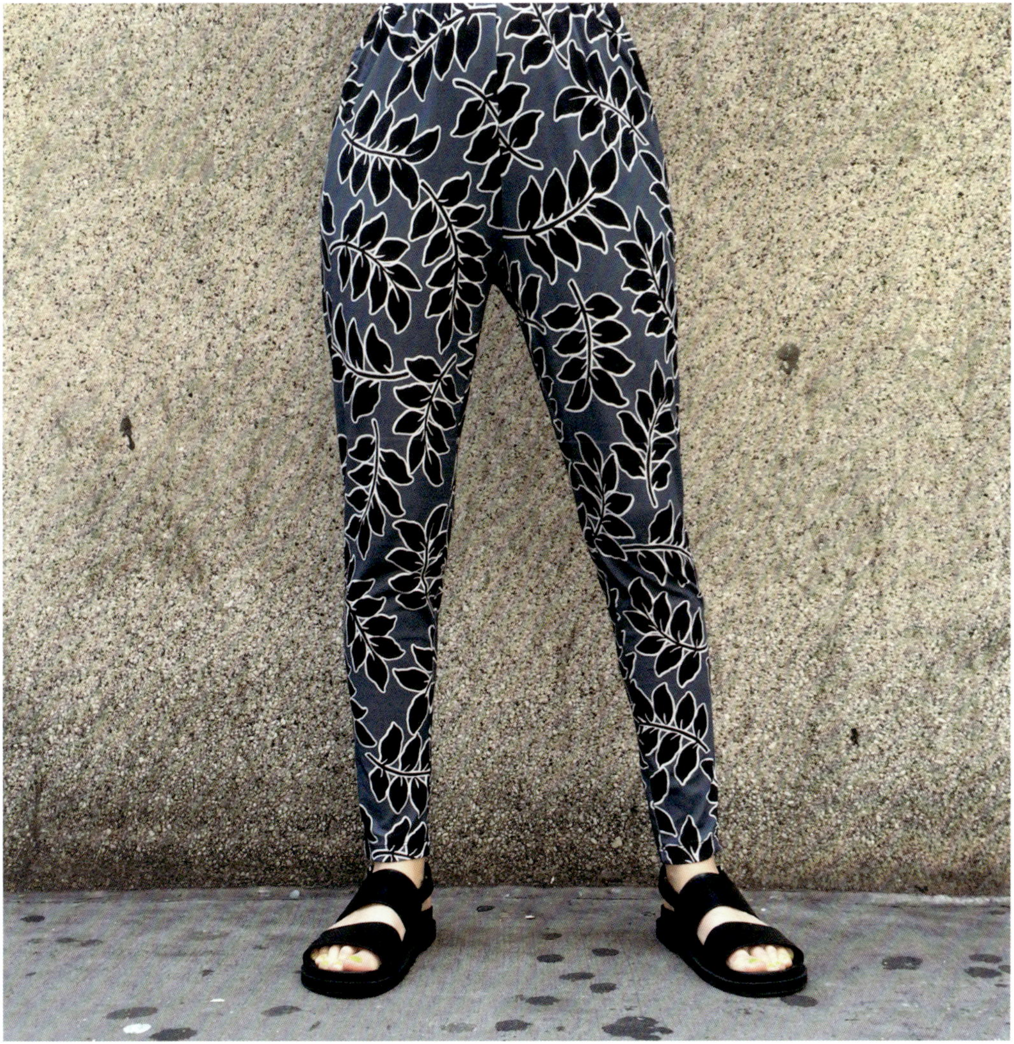

Dyckman St., near Staff St.

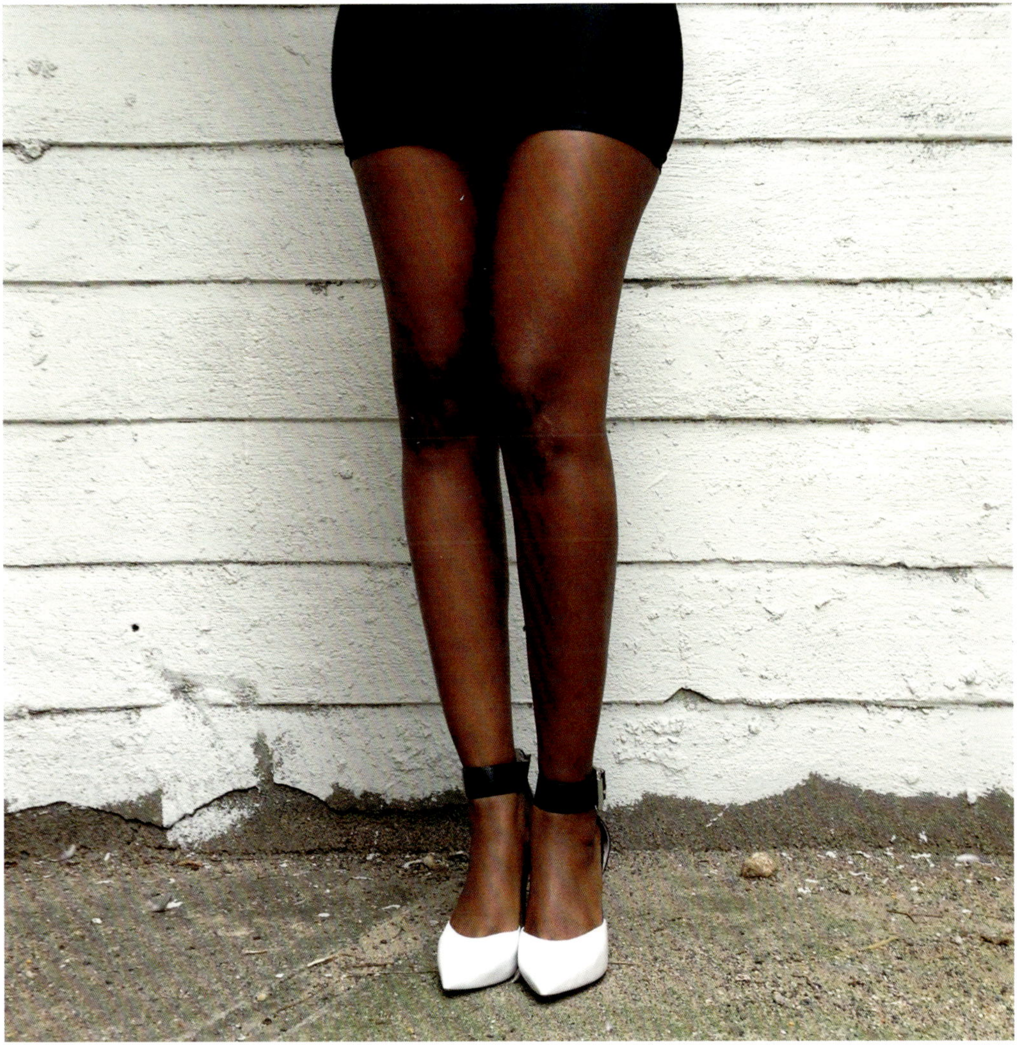

Saint Nicholas Ave. & 125th St.

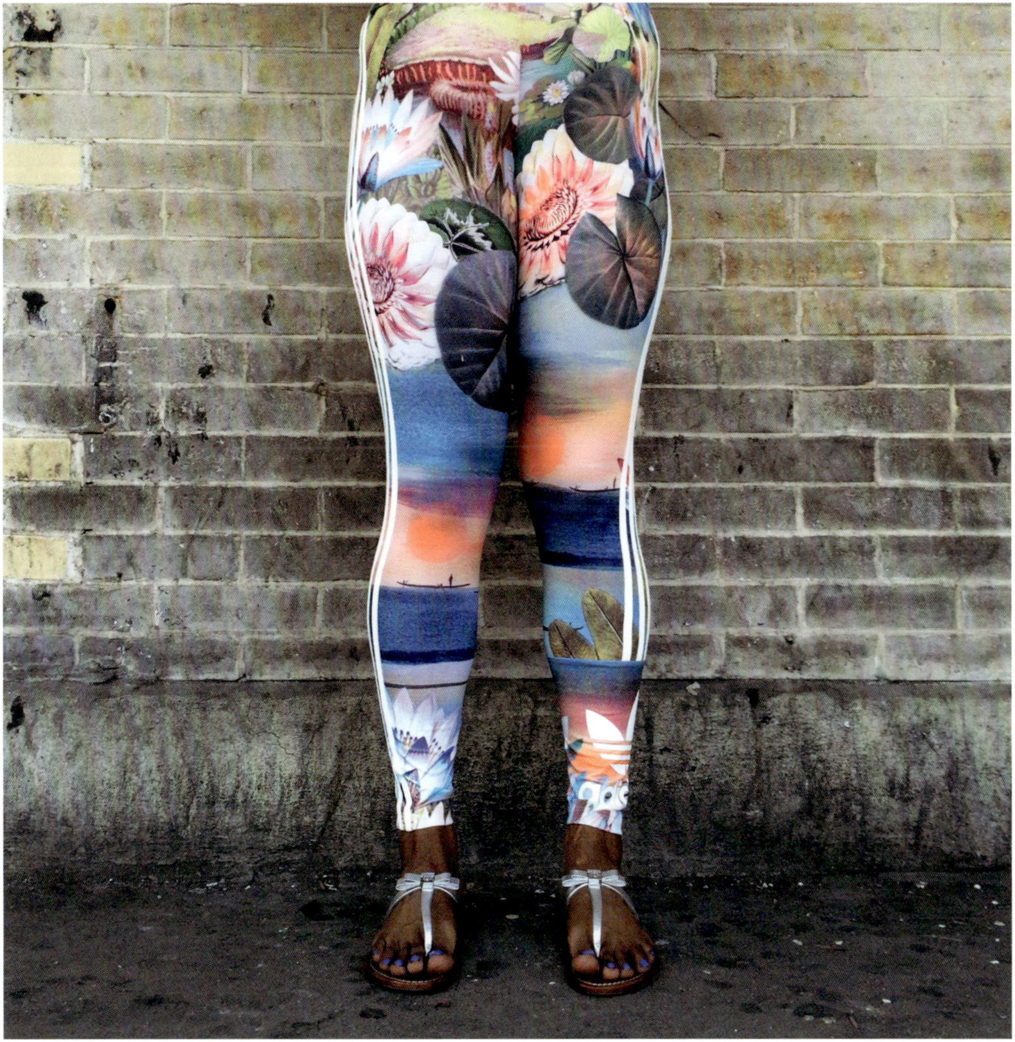

7th Ave., between 42nd & 43rd Sts.

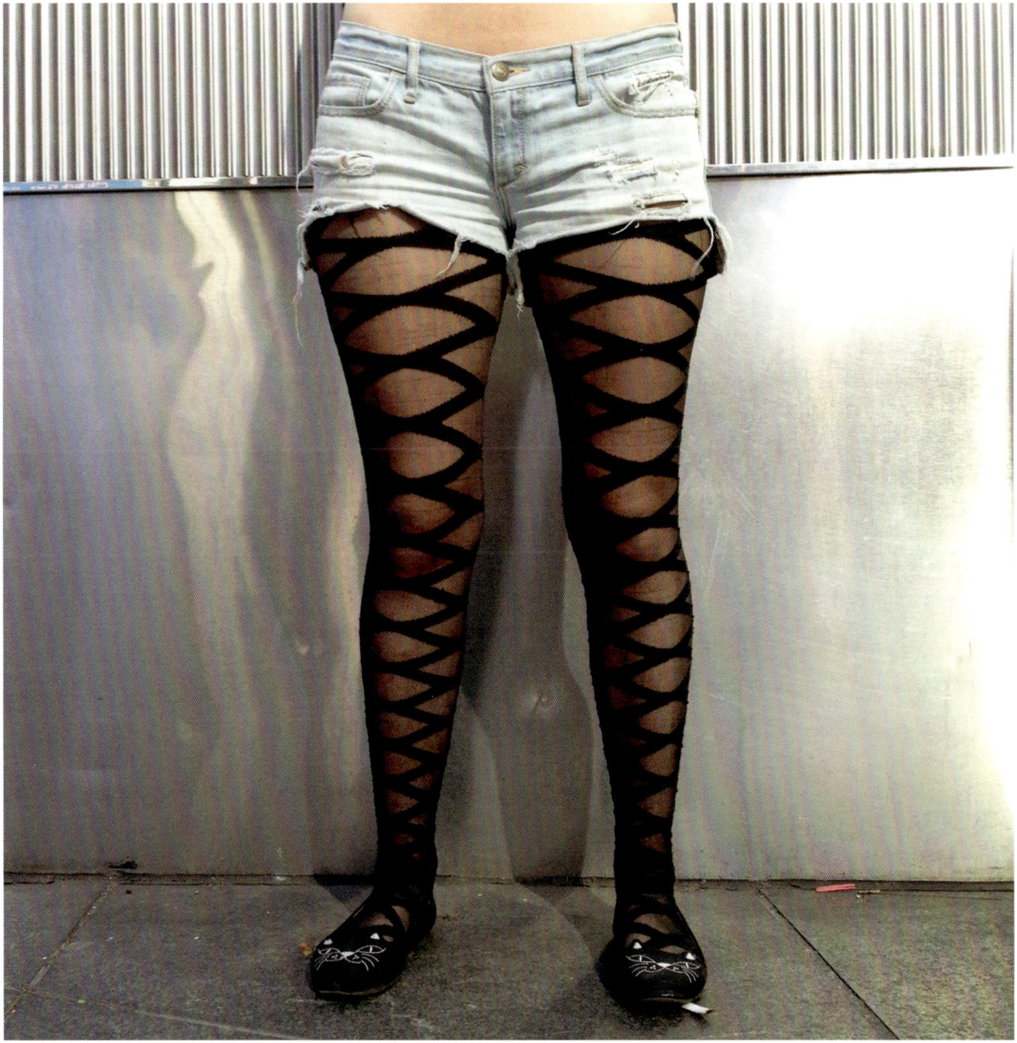

18th St. & Broadway.

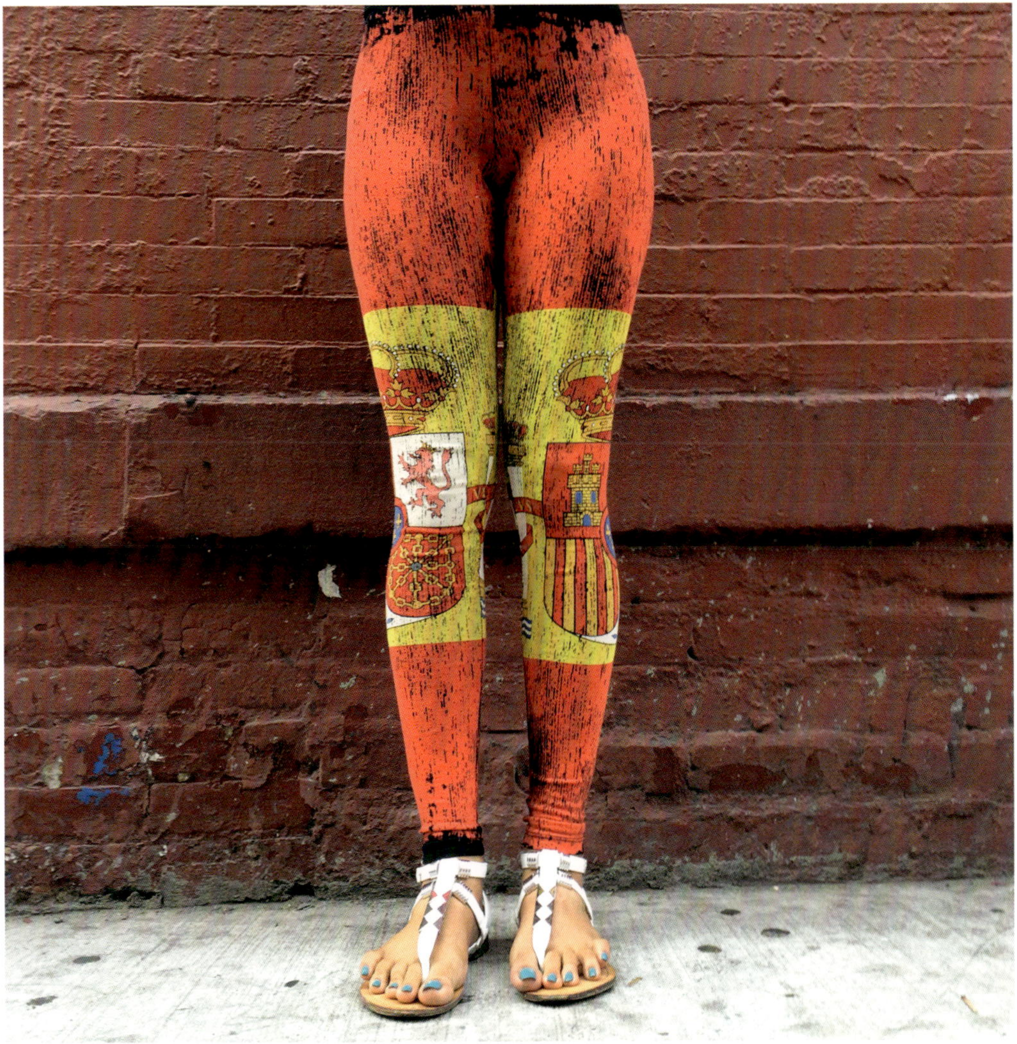

40th St., between 7th & 8th Aves.

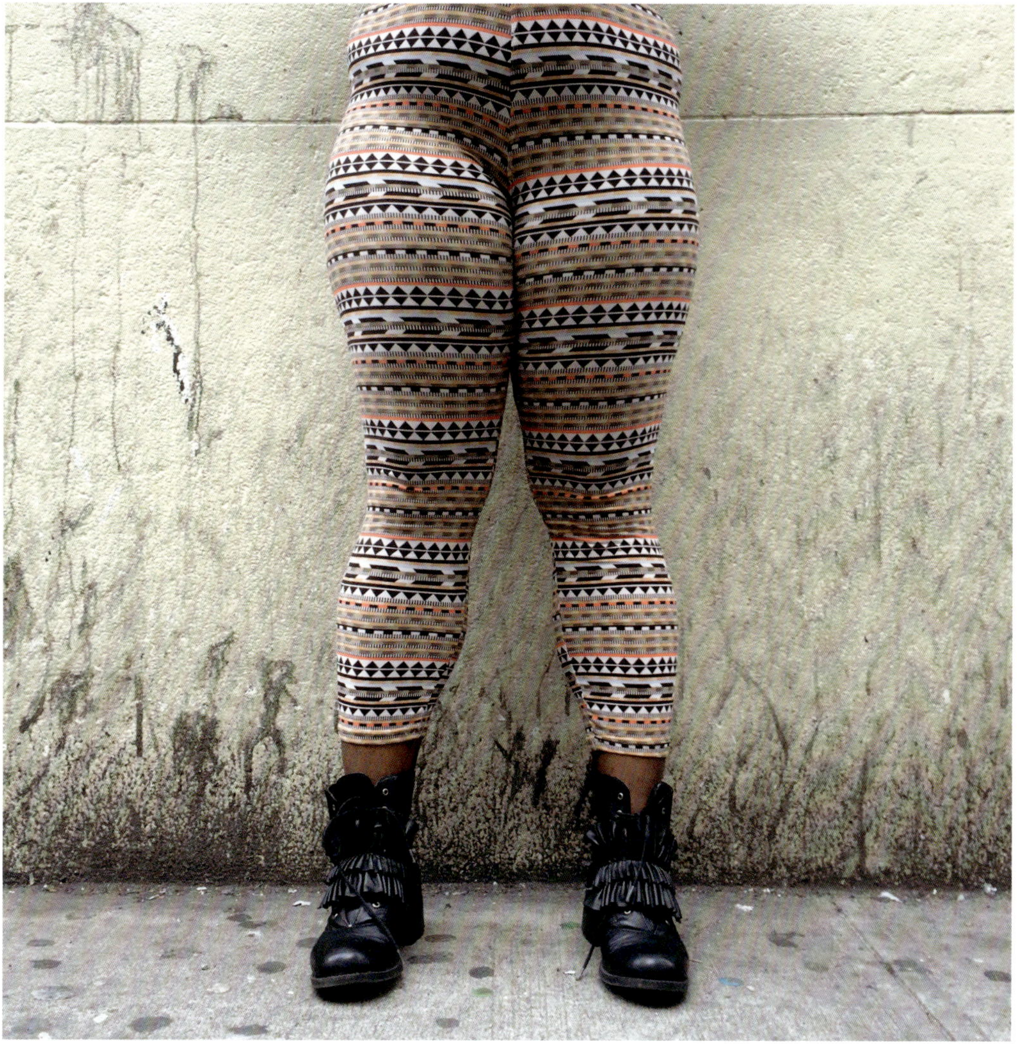

40th St. & 9th Ave.

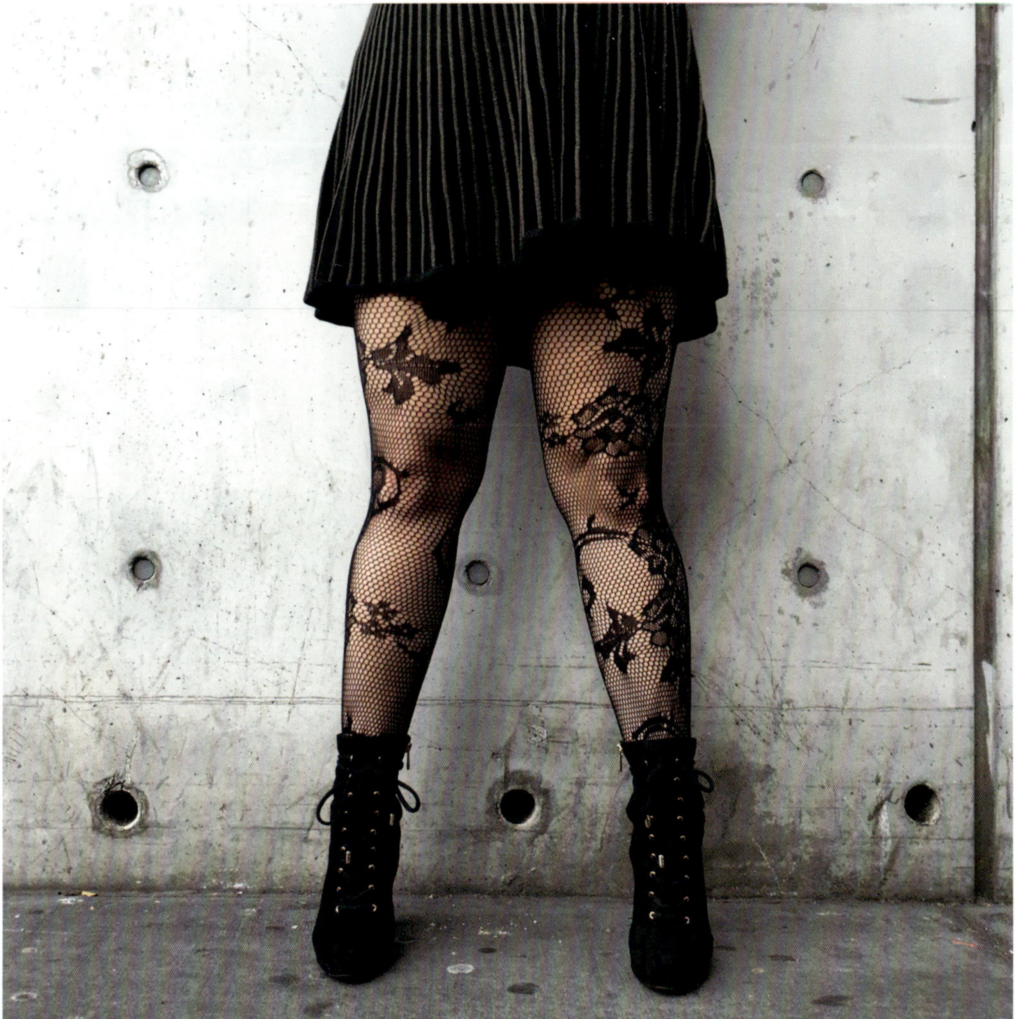

40th St., between 7th & 8th Aves.

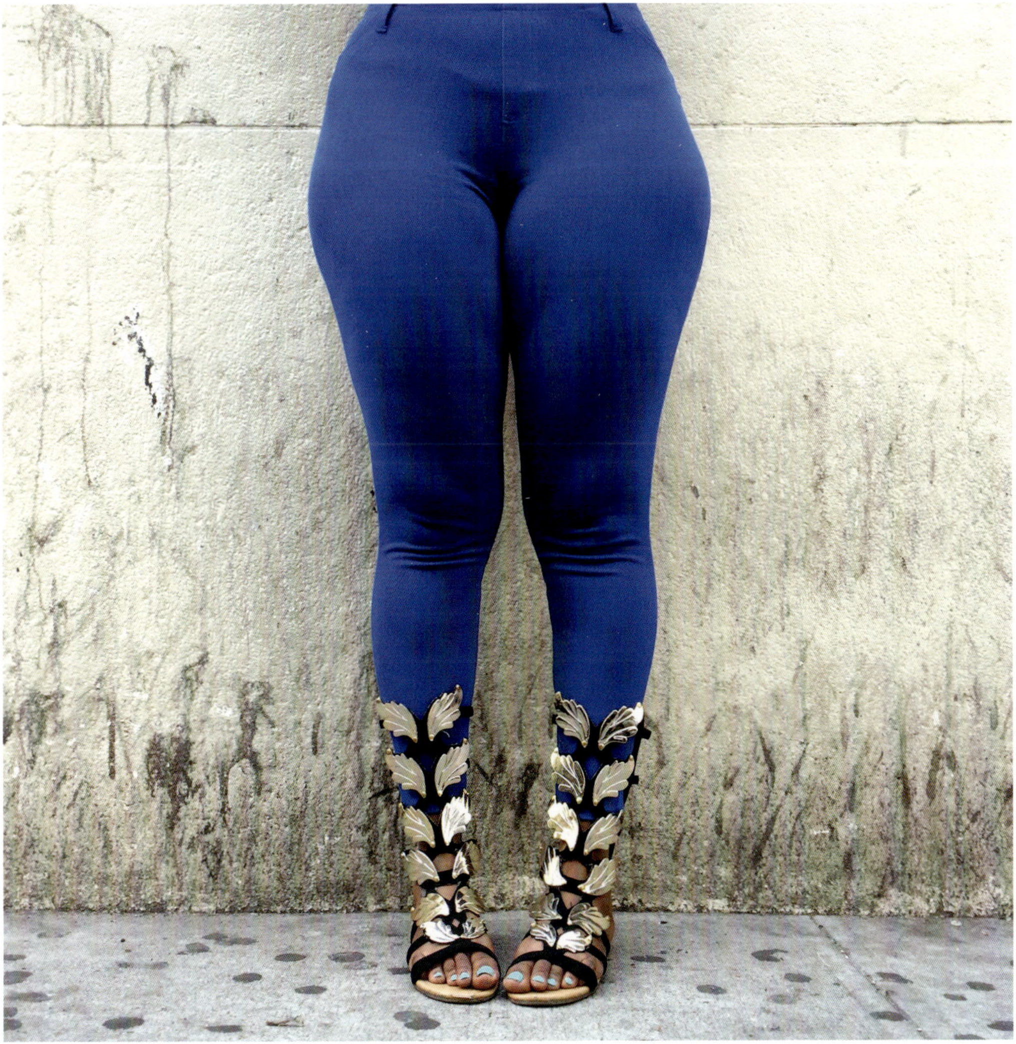

4th St., near 6th Ave.

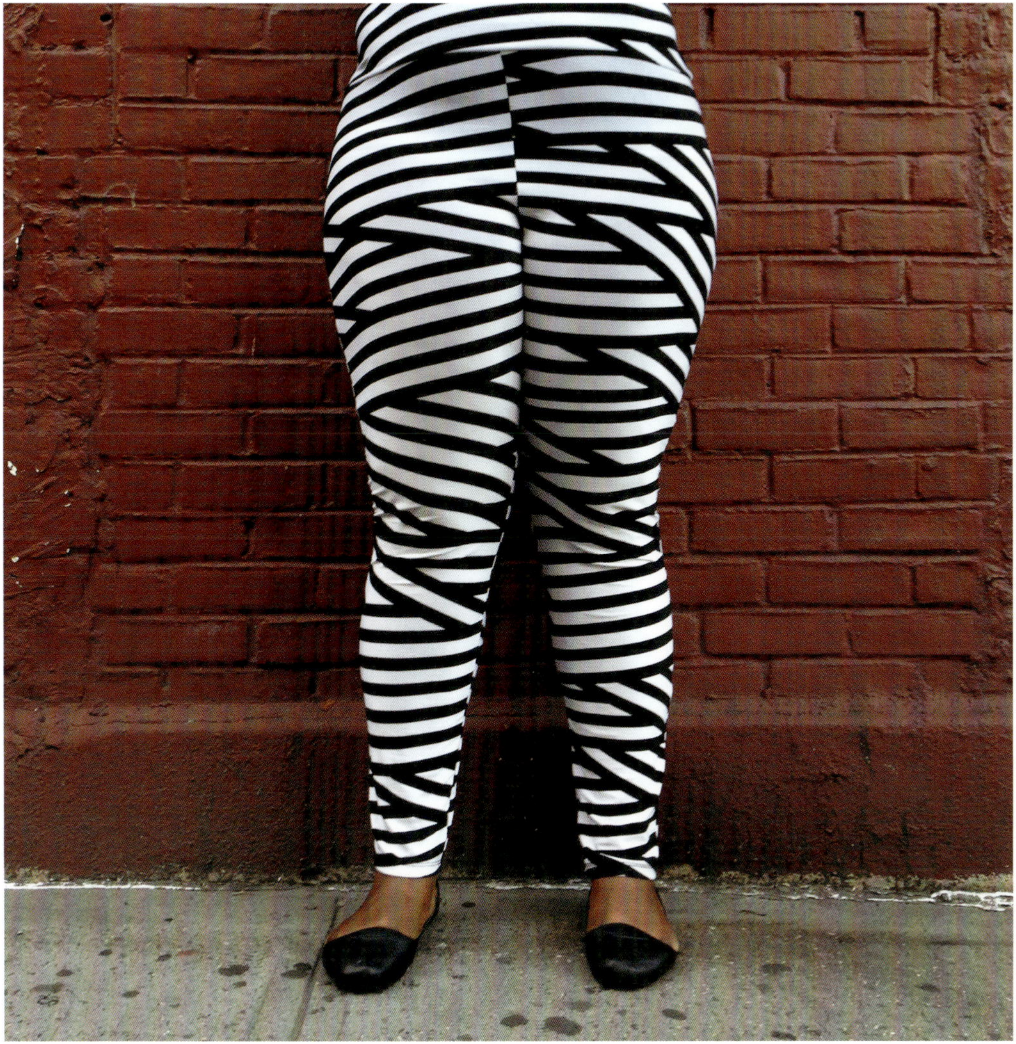

125th St. & Adam Clayton Powell Jr. Blvd.

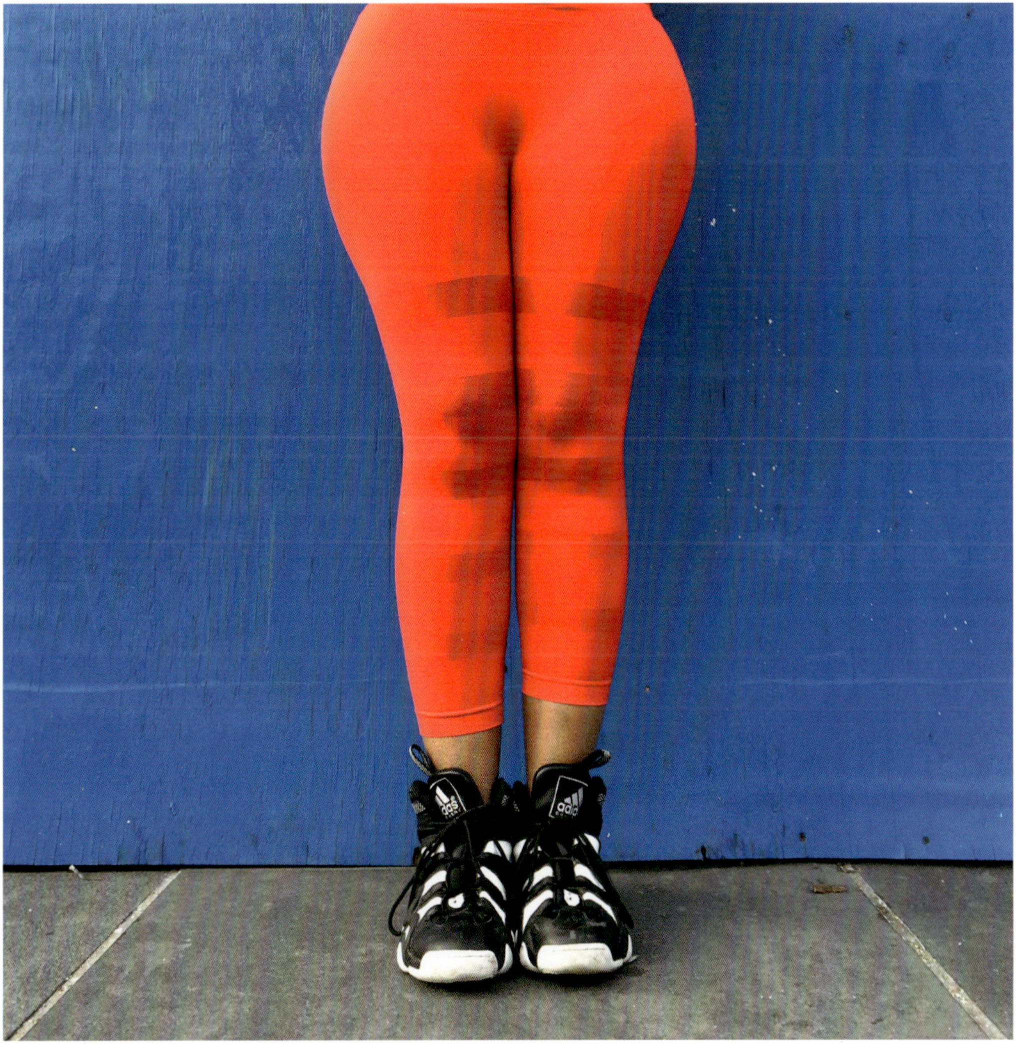

40th St., between 5th & 6th Aves.

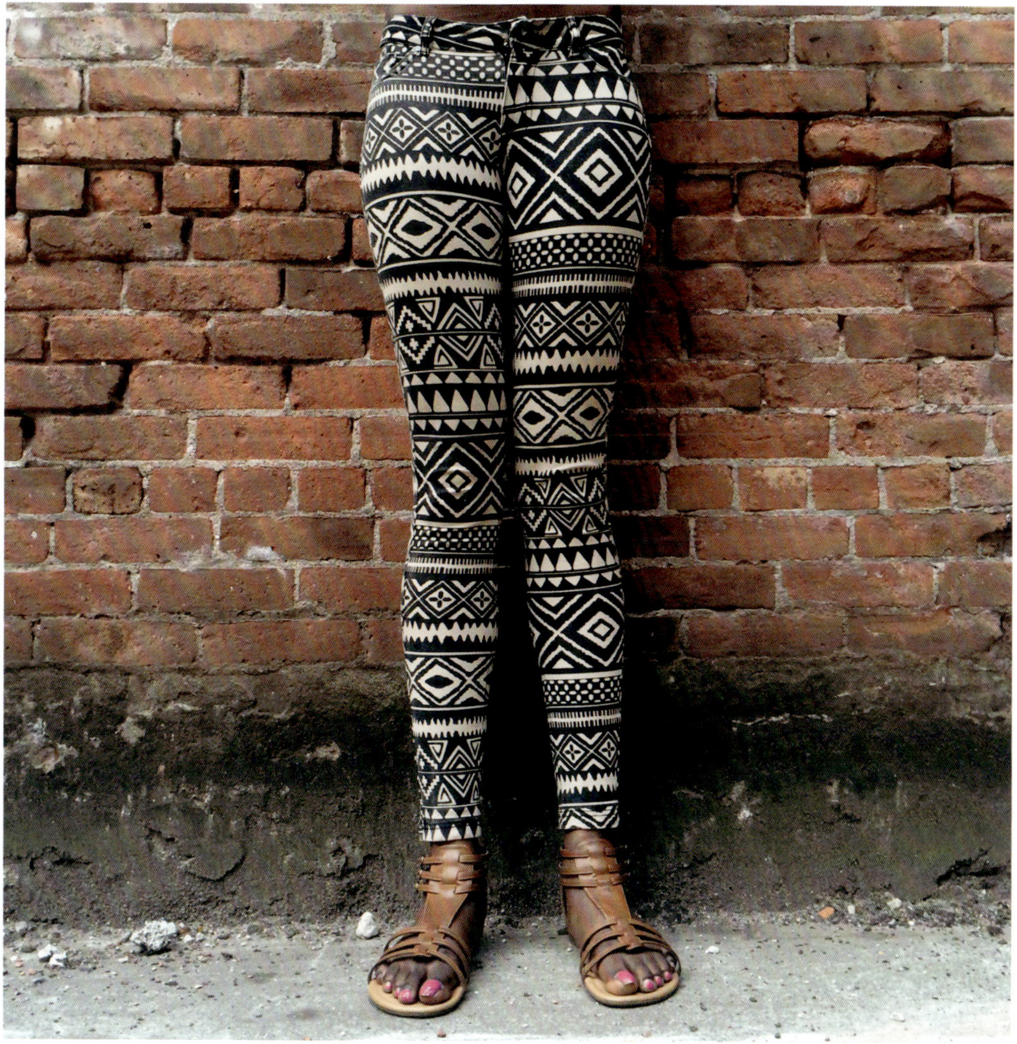

125th St. & Lexington Ave.

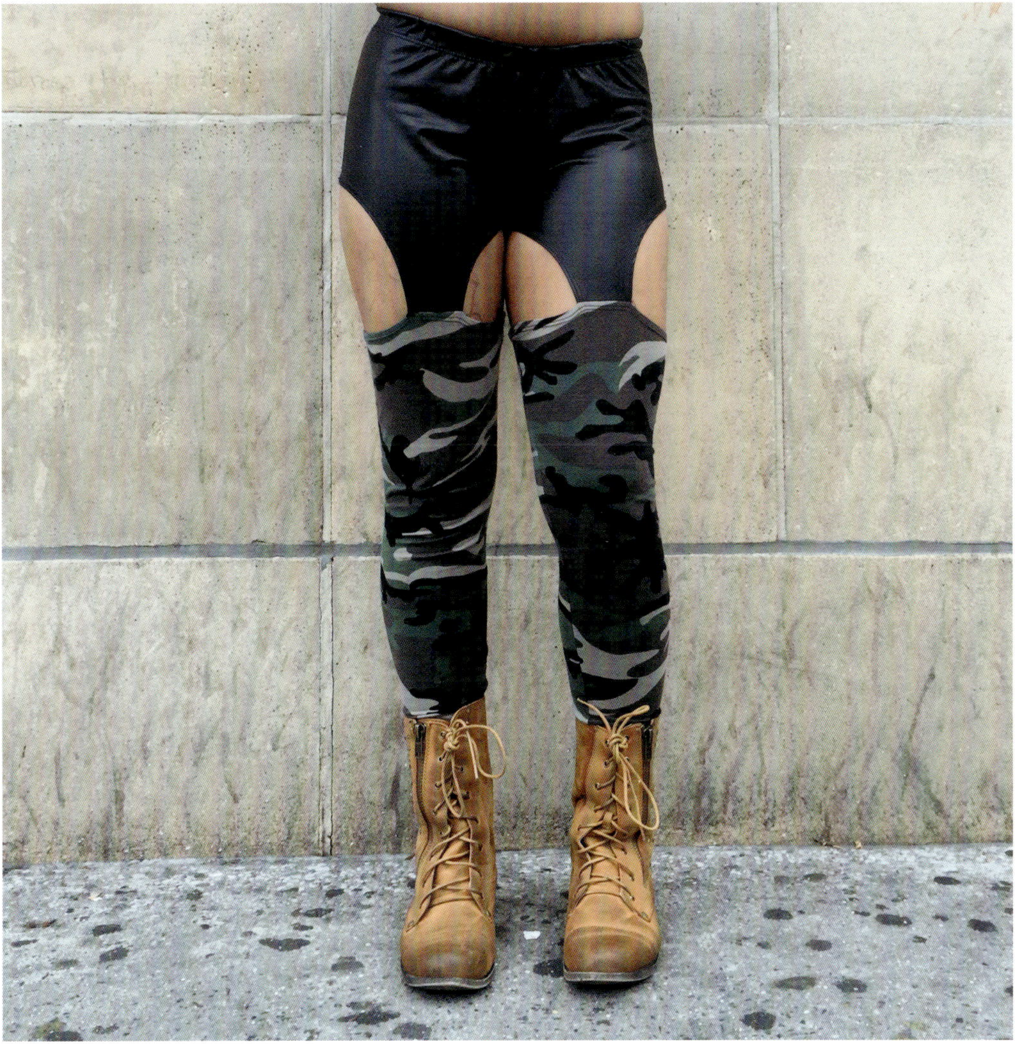

77th St. & 5th Ave.

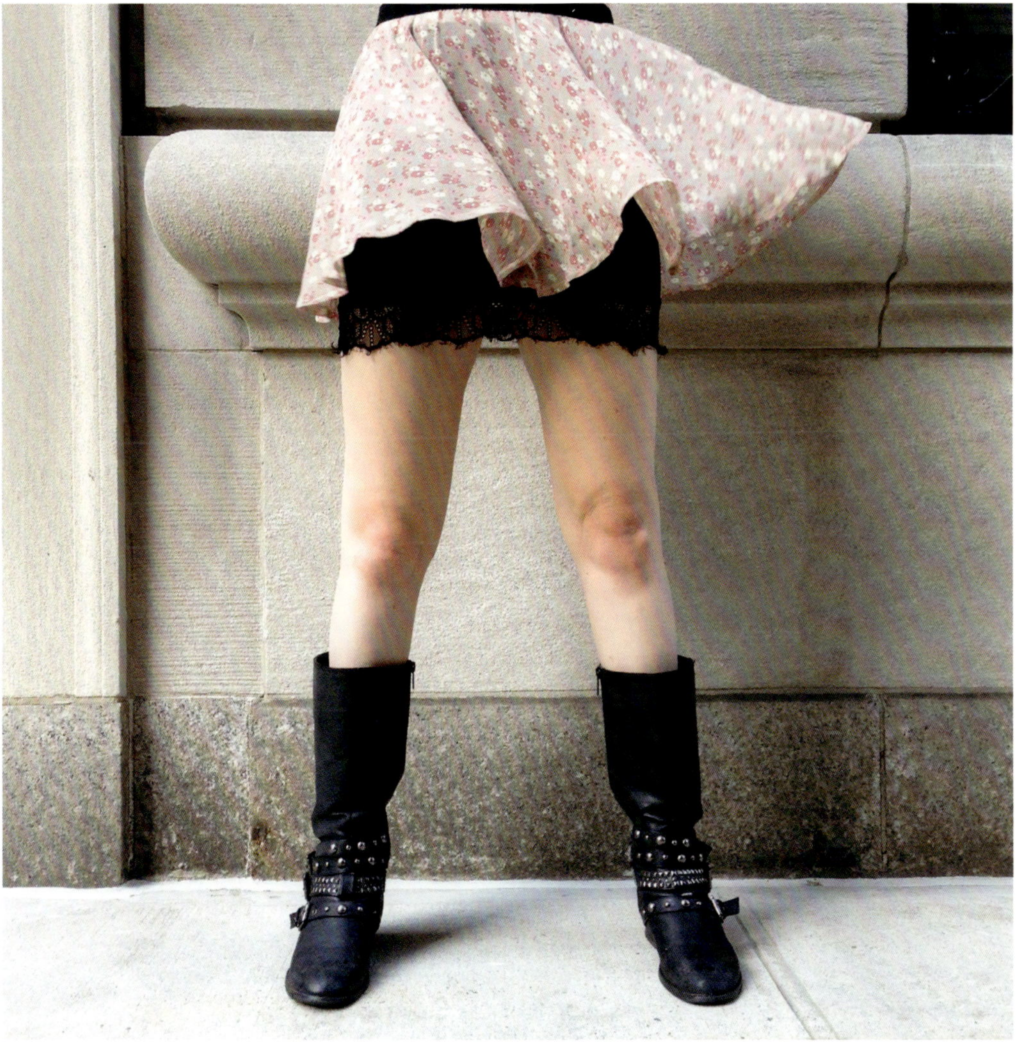

Saint Nicholas Ave. & 125th St.

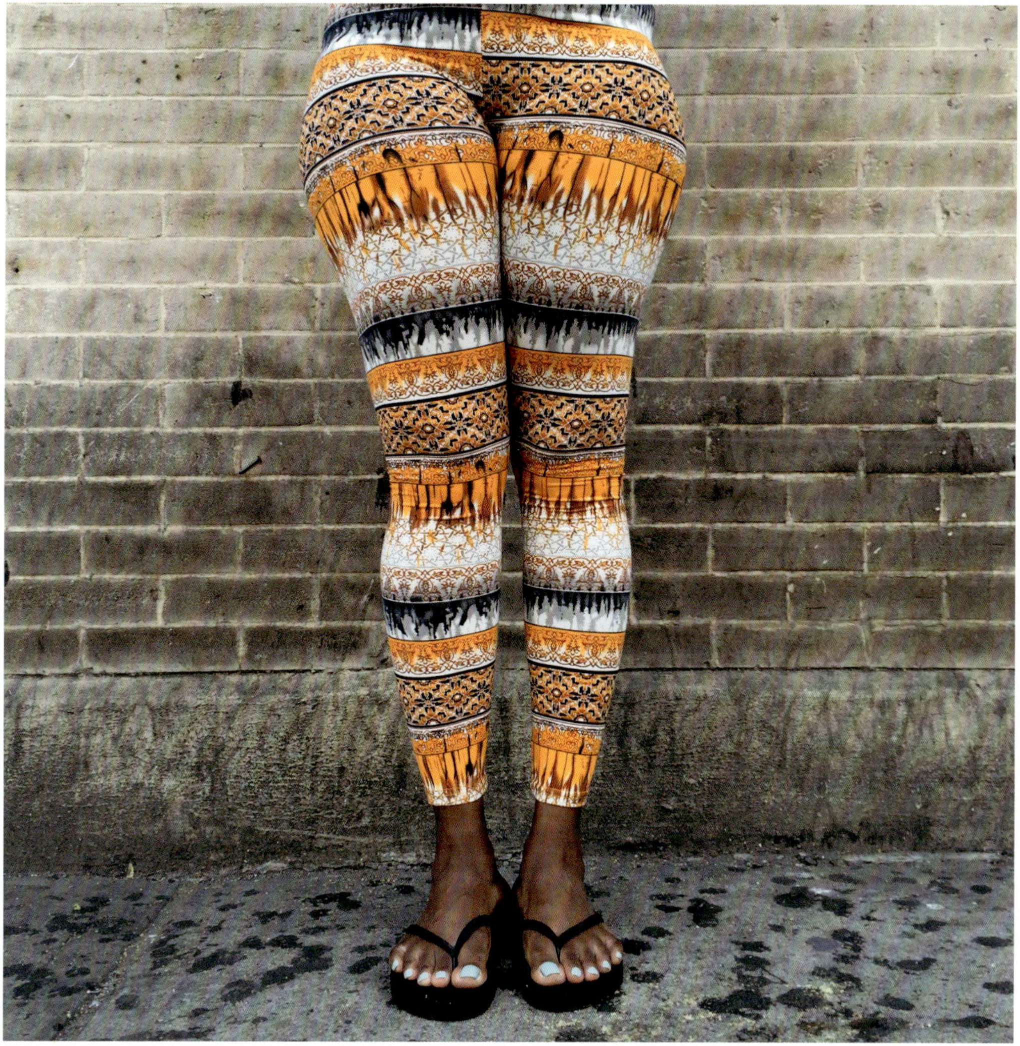

40th St., between 7th & 8th Aves.

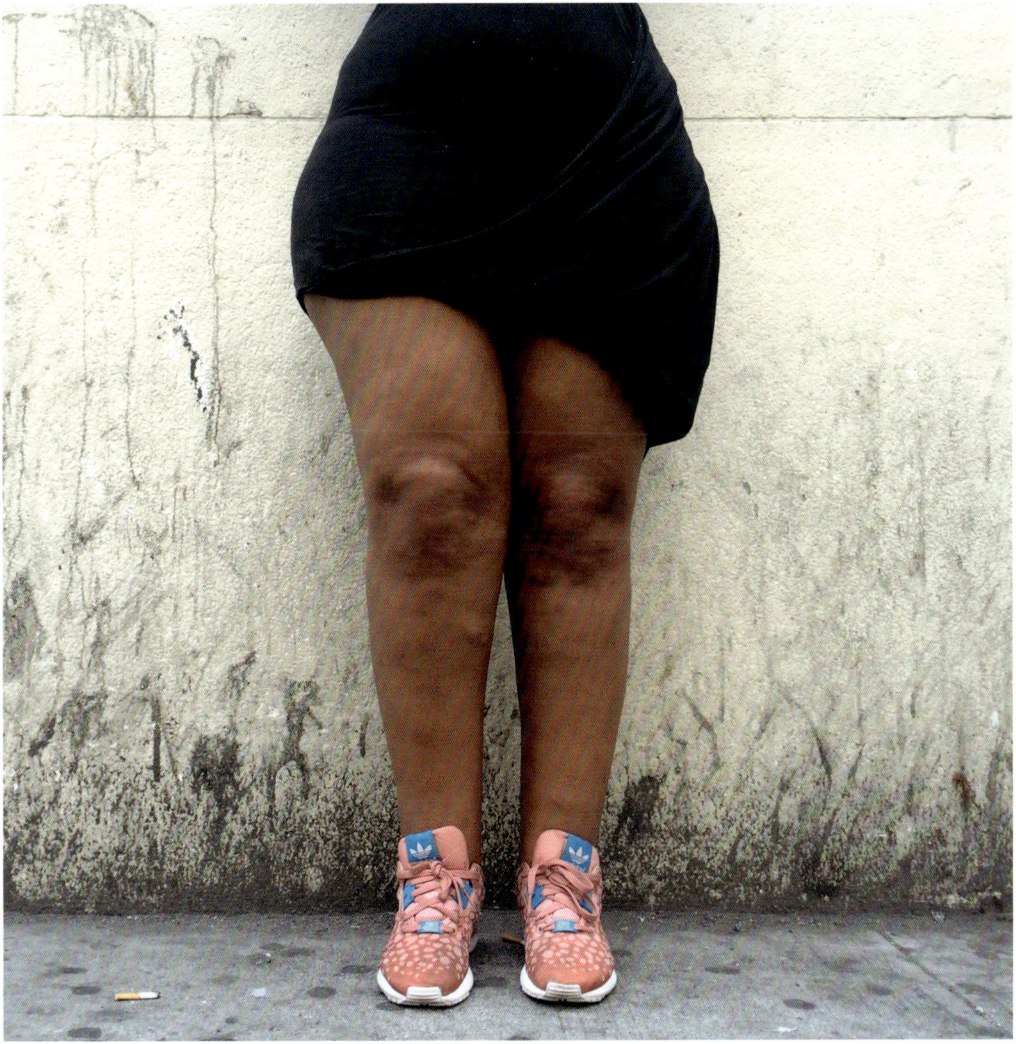

125th St. & Saint Nicholas Ave.

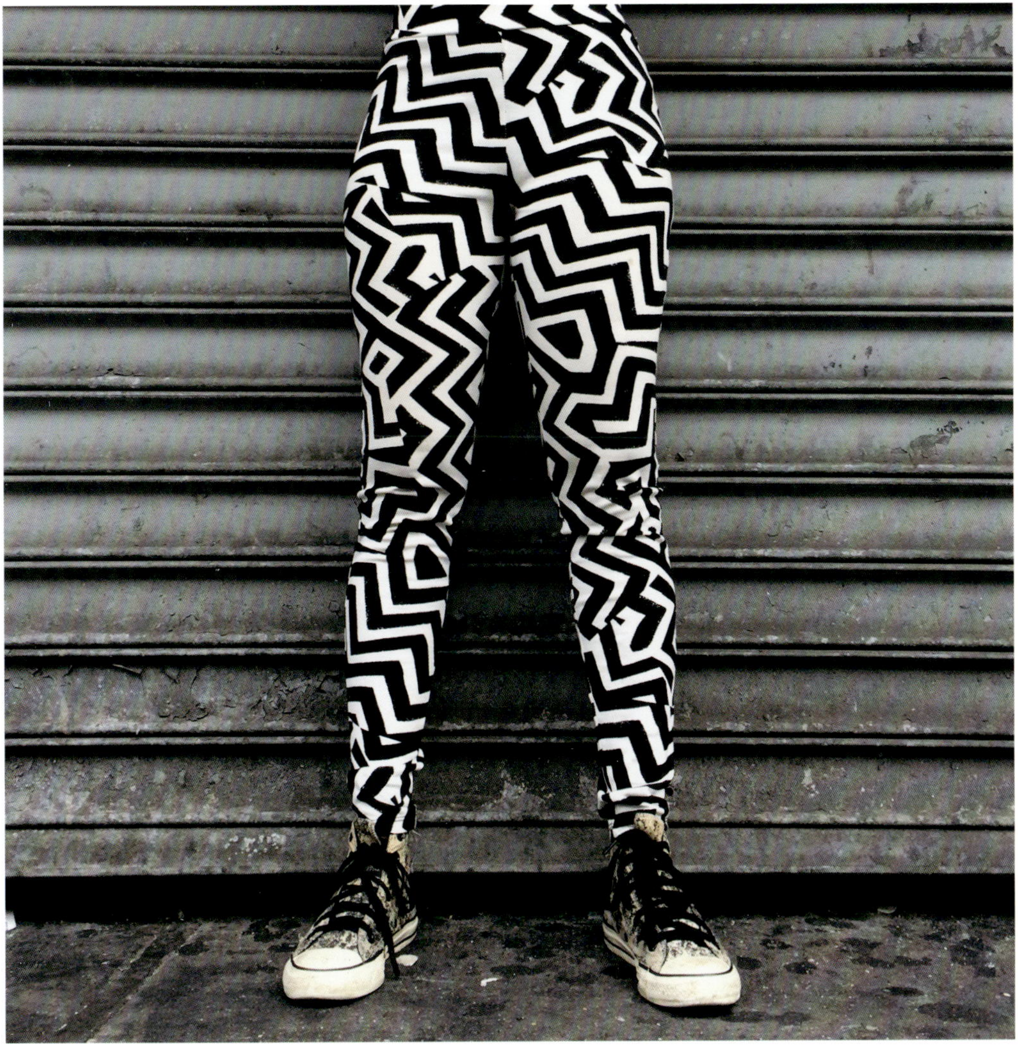

40th St., between 7th & 8th Aves.

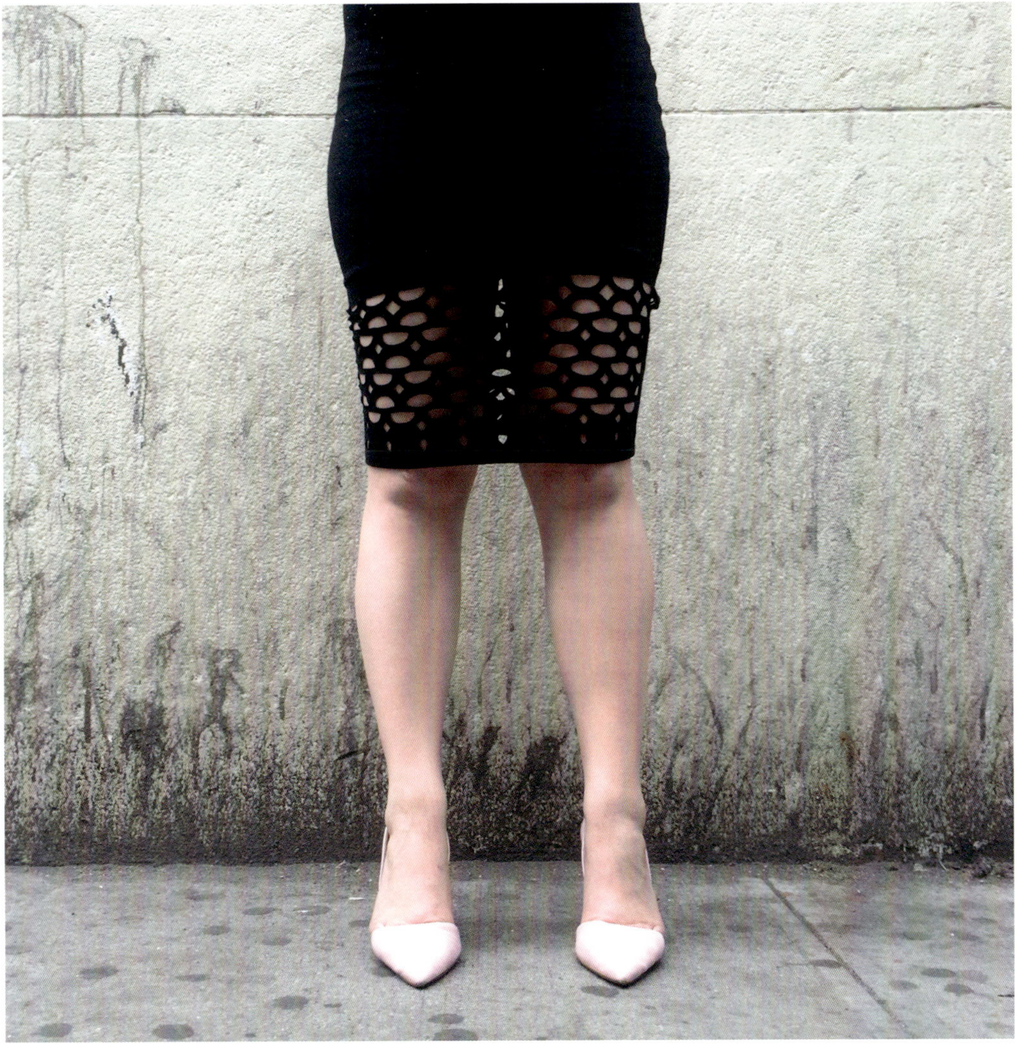

Prince & Mercer Sts.

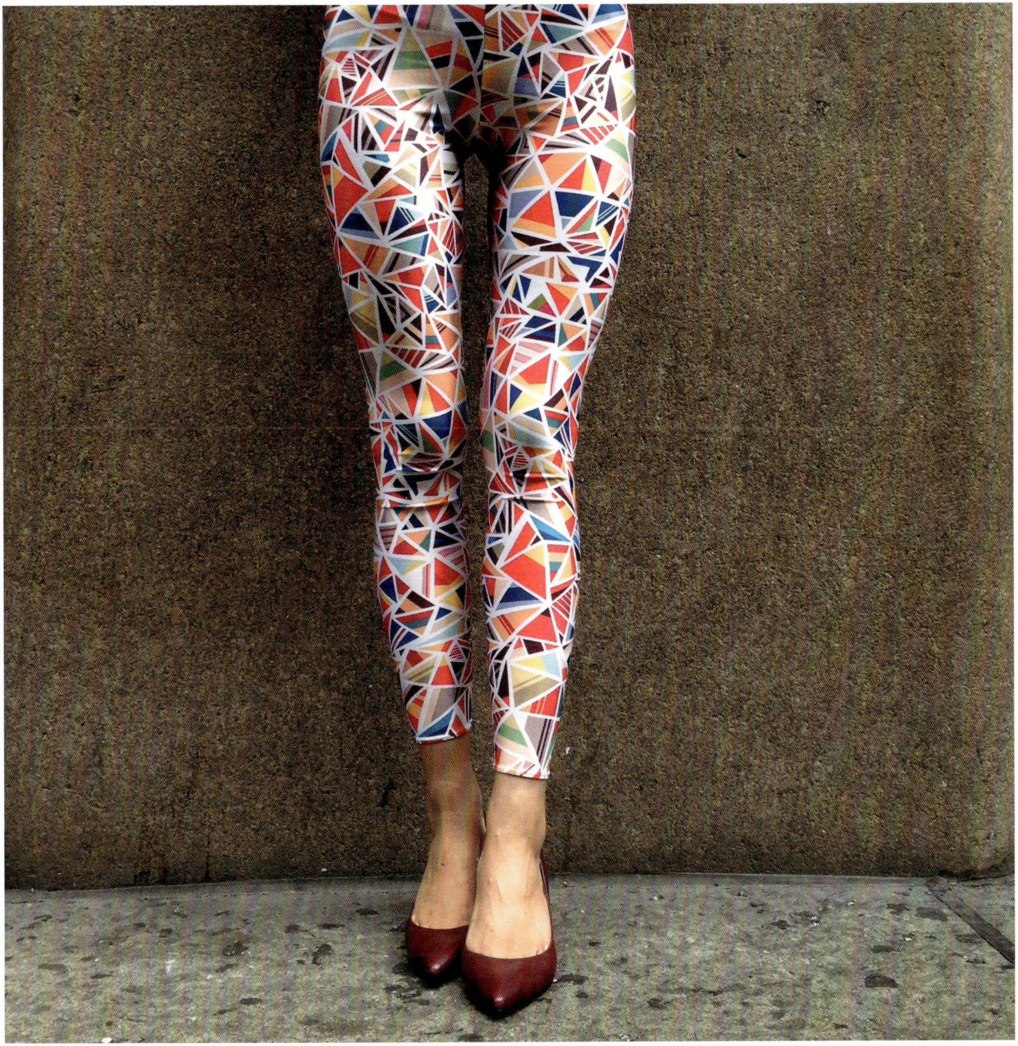

40th St., between 7th & 8th Aves.

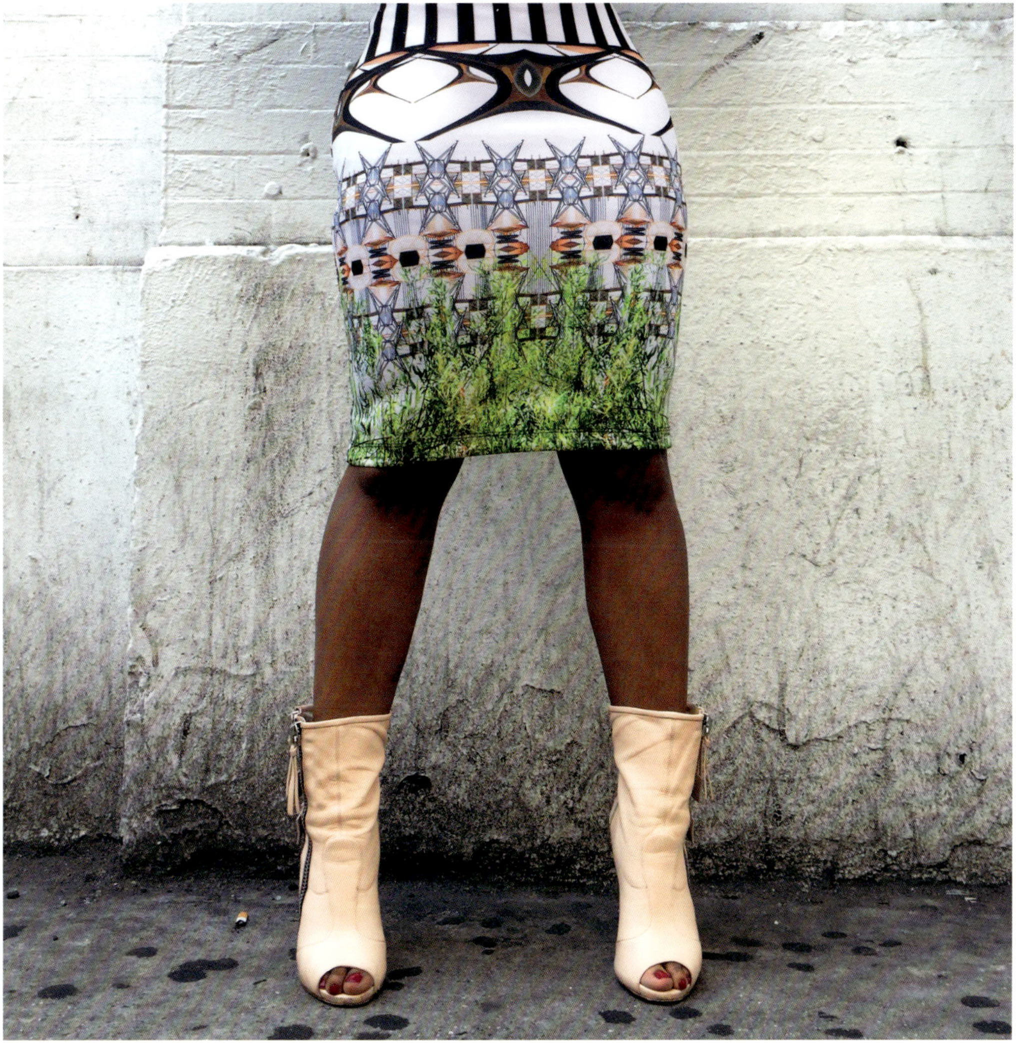

39th St. & 8th Ave.

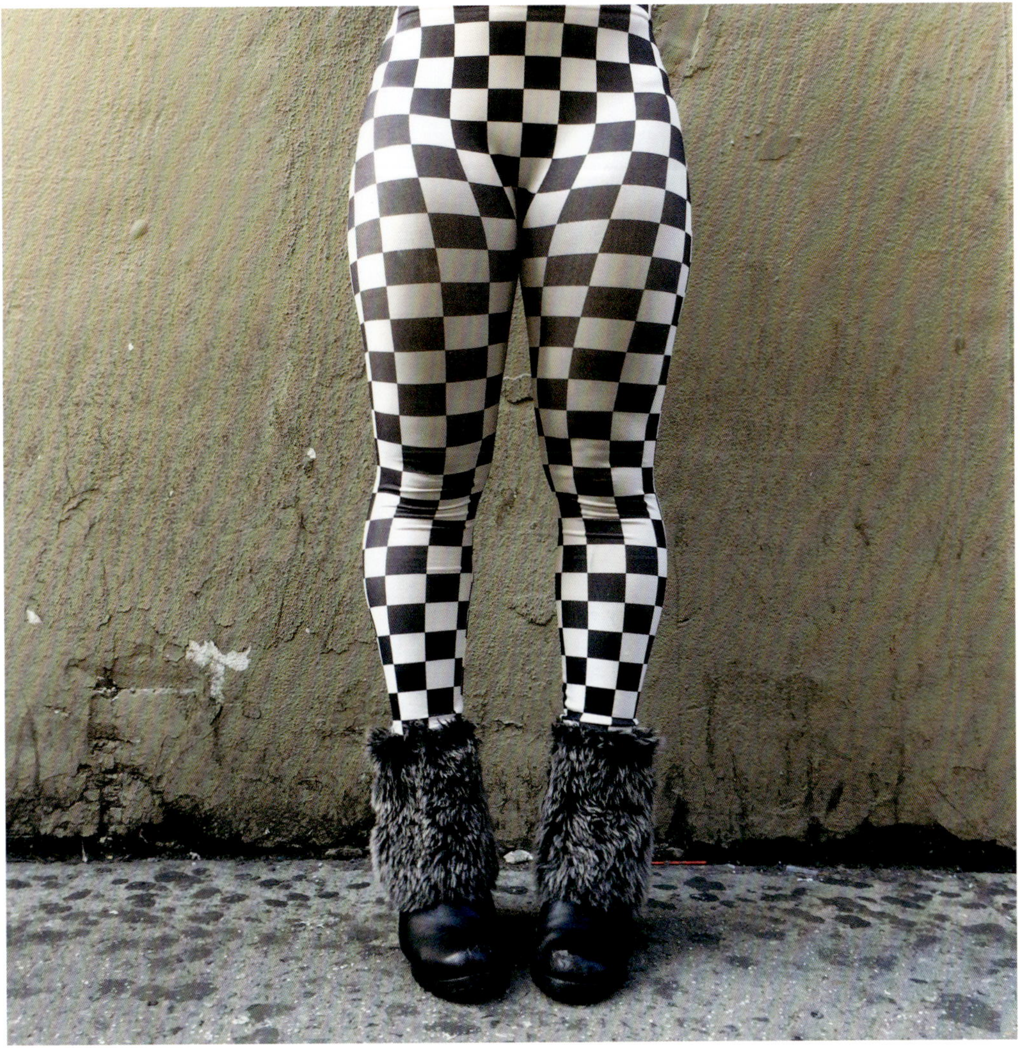

16th St., near 5th Ave.

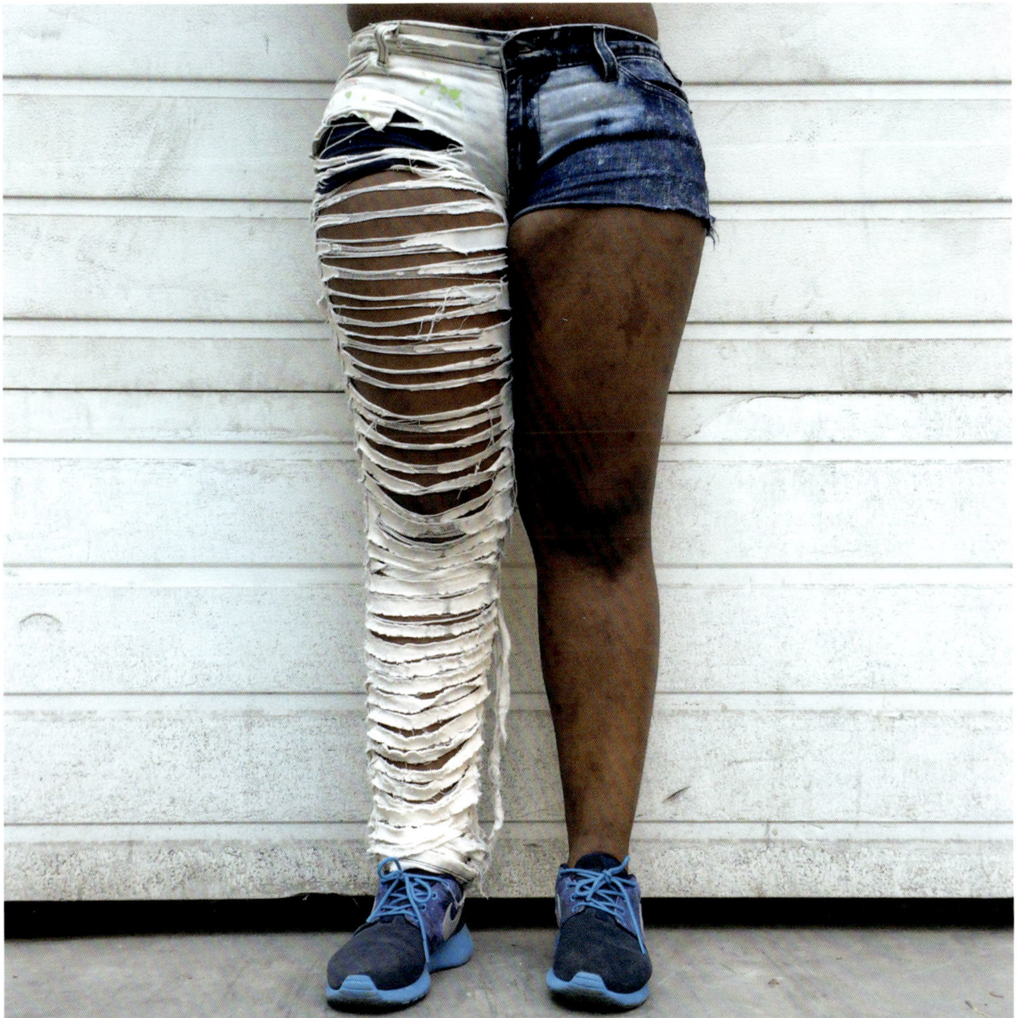

125th St. & Lexington Ave.

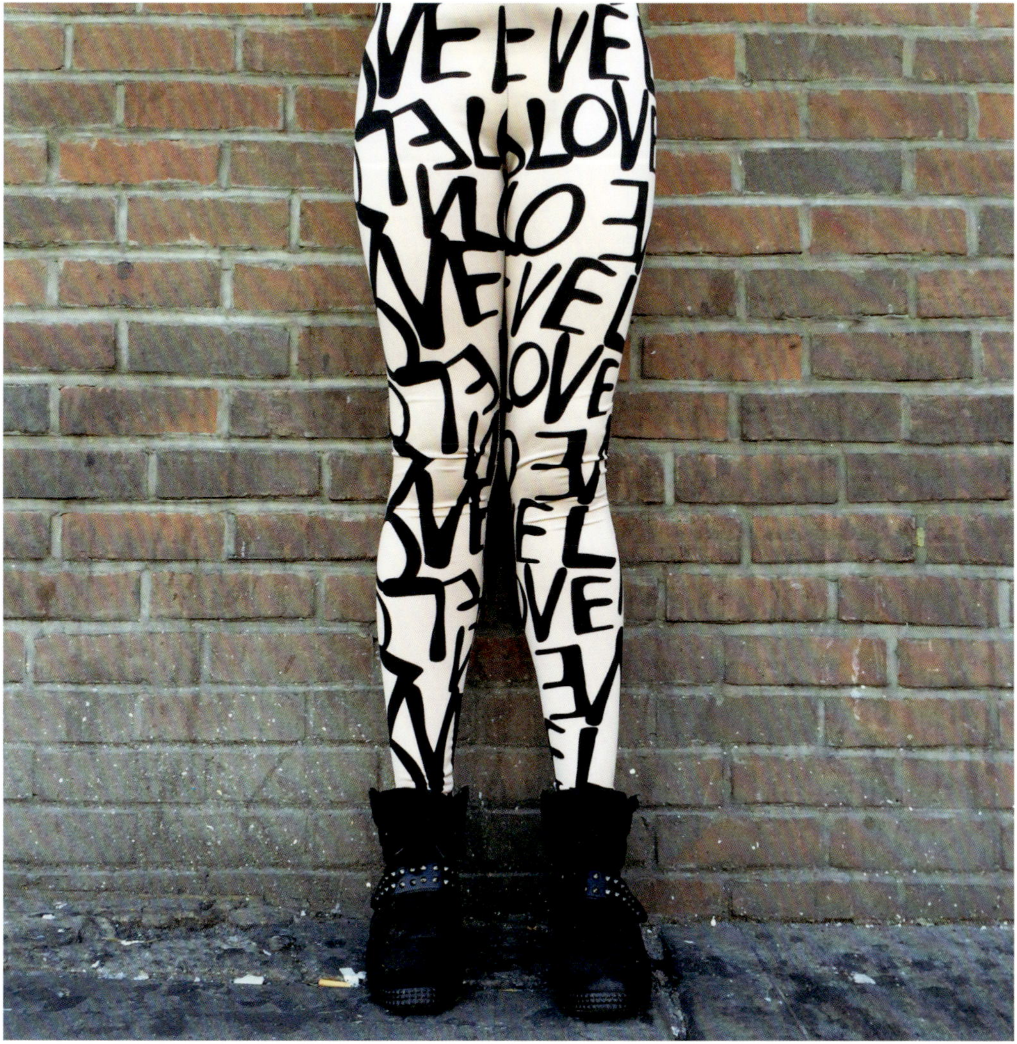

Mott & Prince Sts.

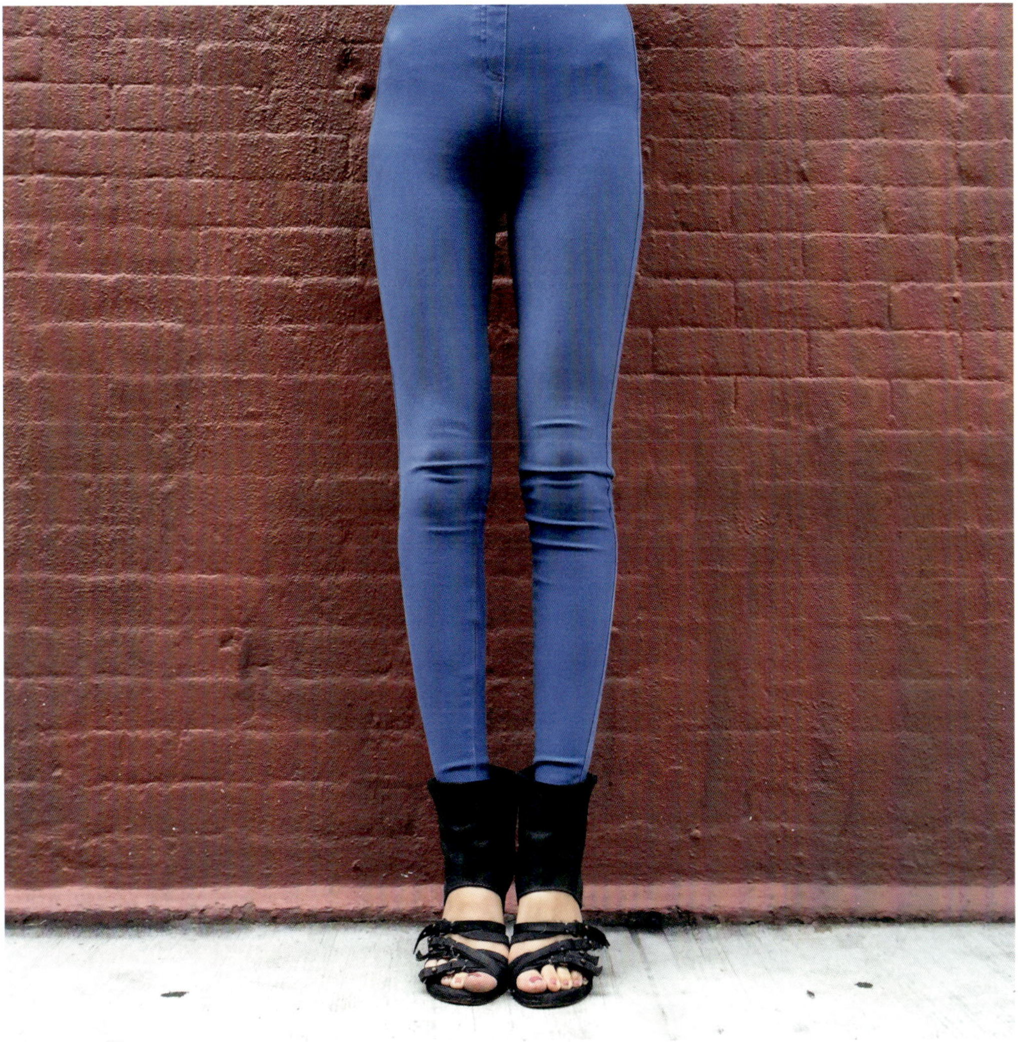

8th Ave. & 42nd St.

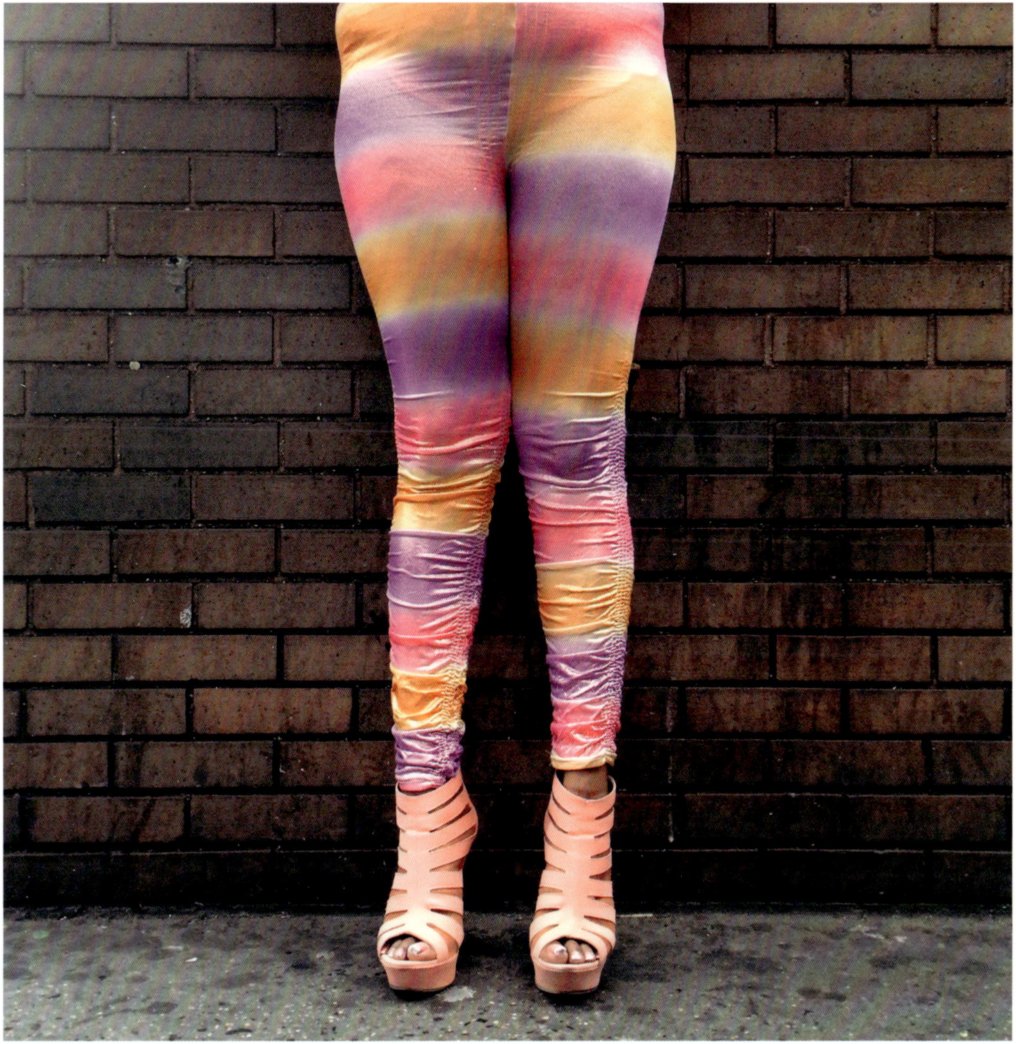

40th St., between 7th & 8th Aves.

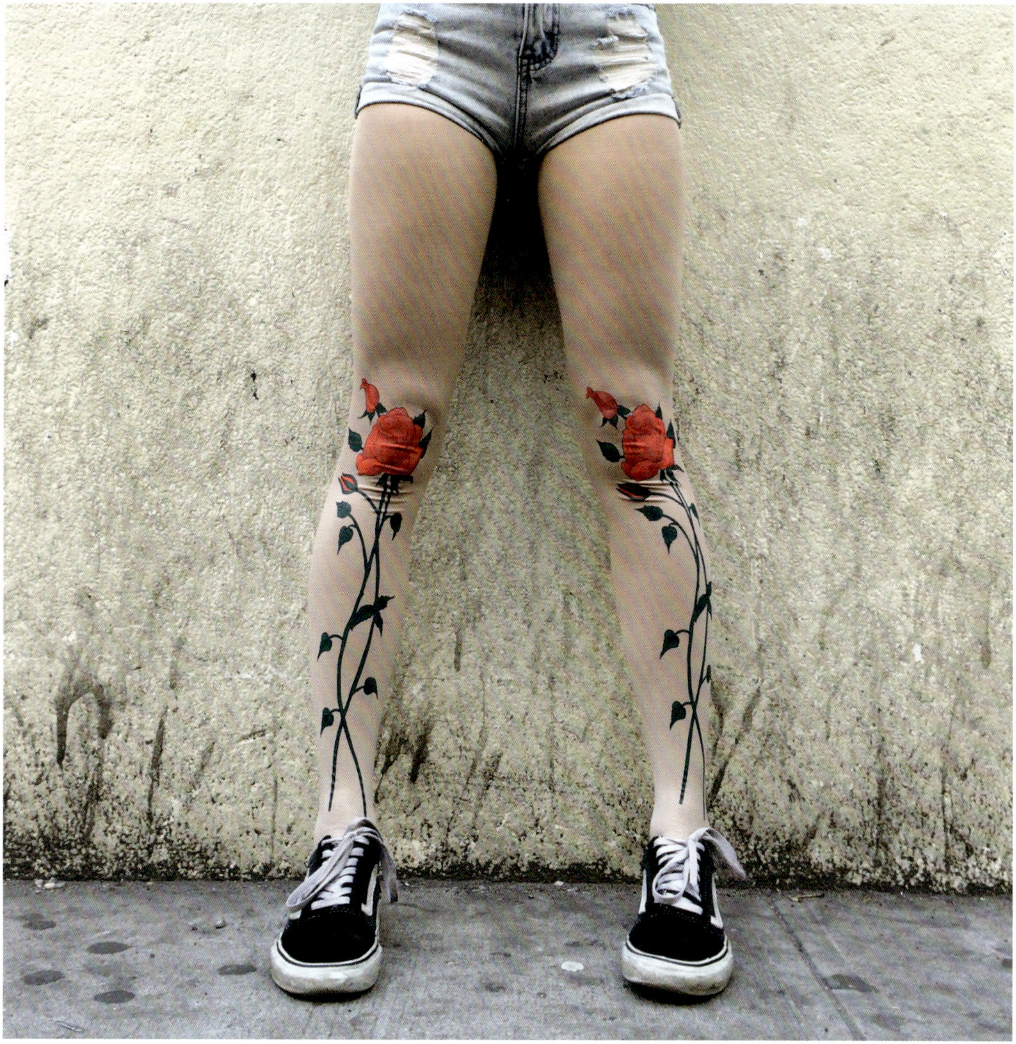

University Place & 14th St.

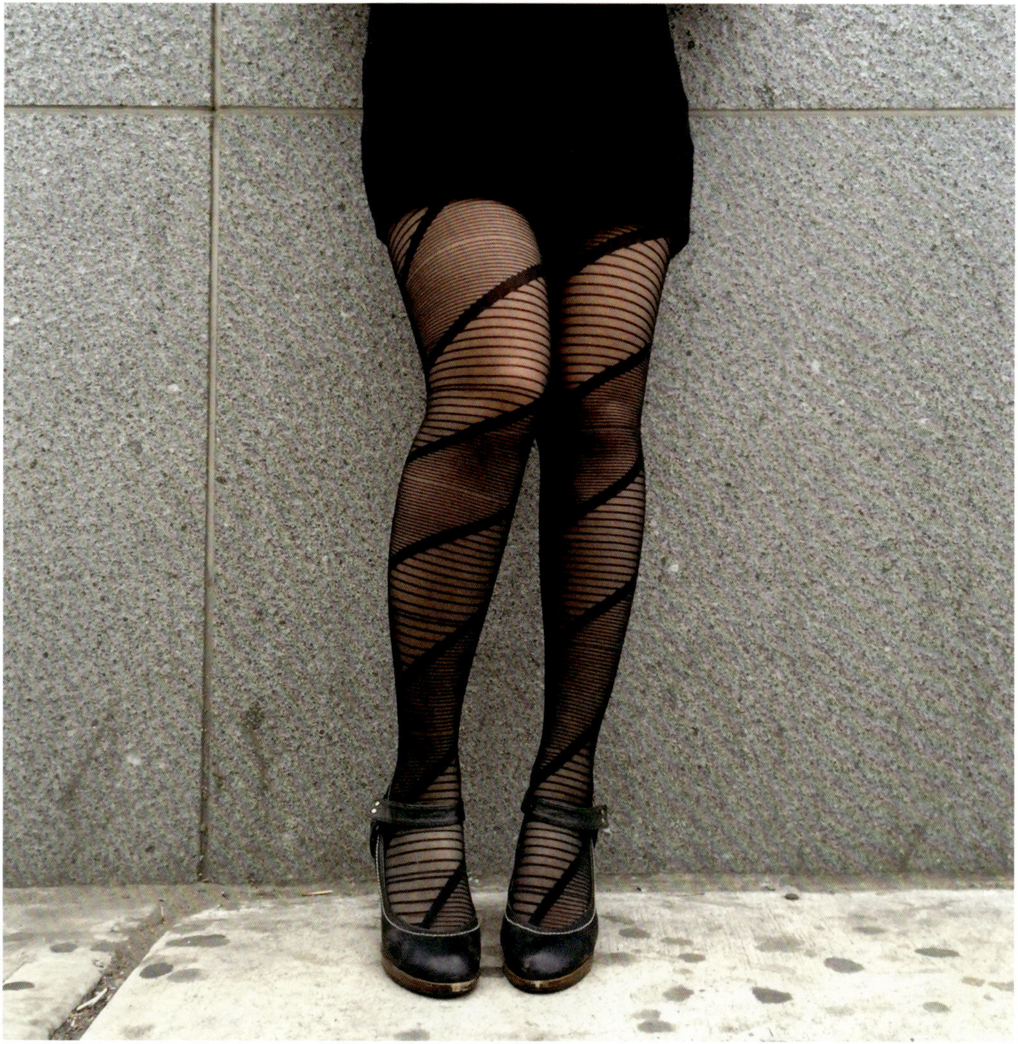

Mulberry & Spring Sts.

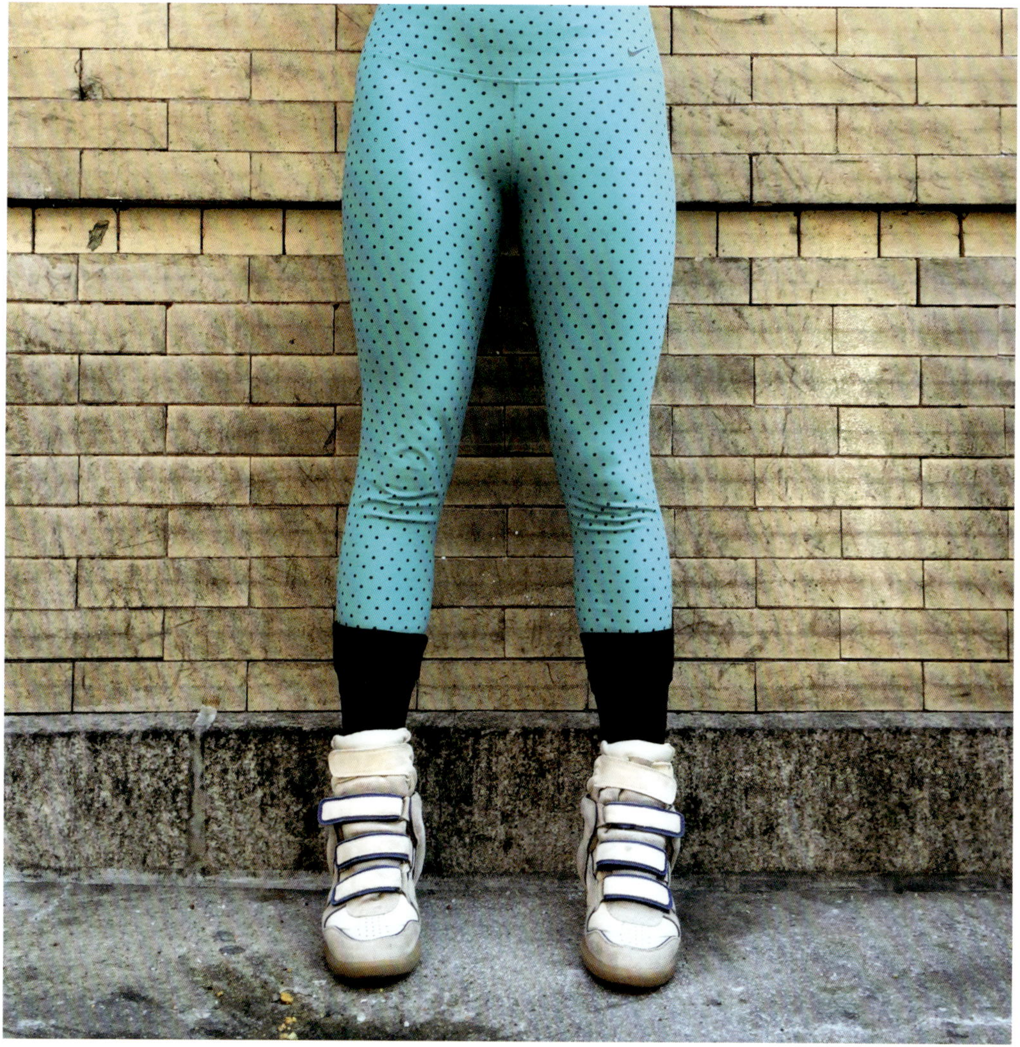

Madison Ave. & 61st St.

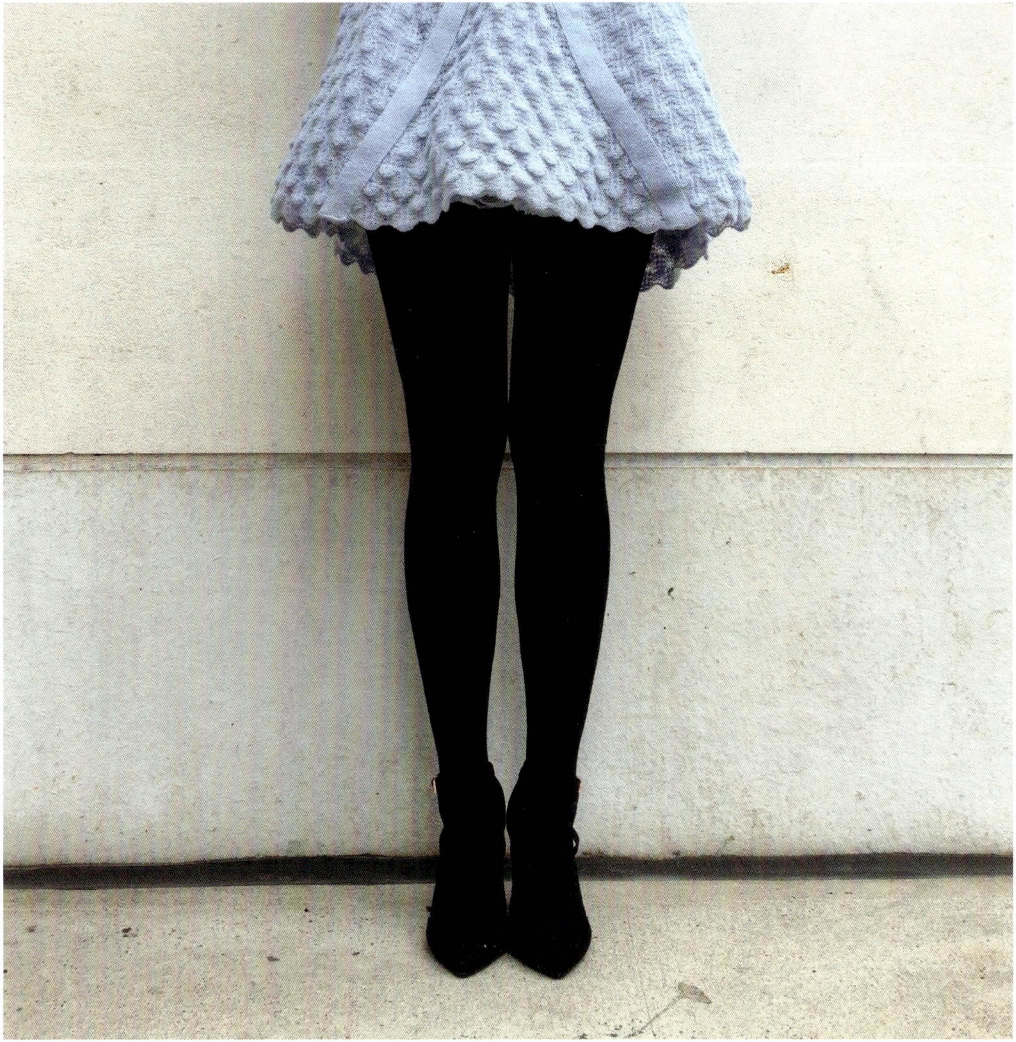

40th St., near 8th Ave.

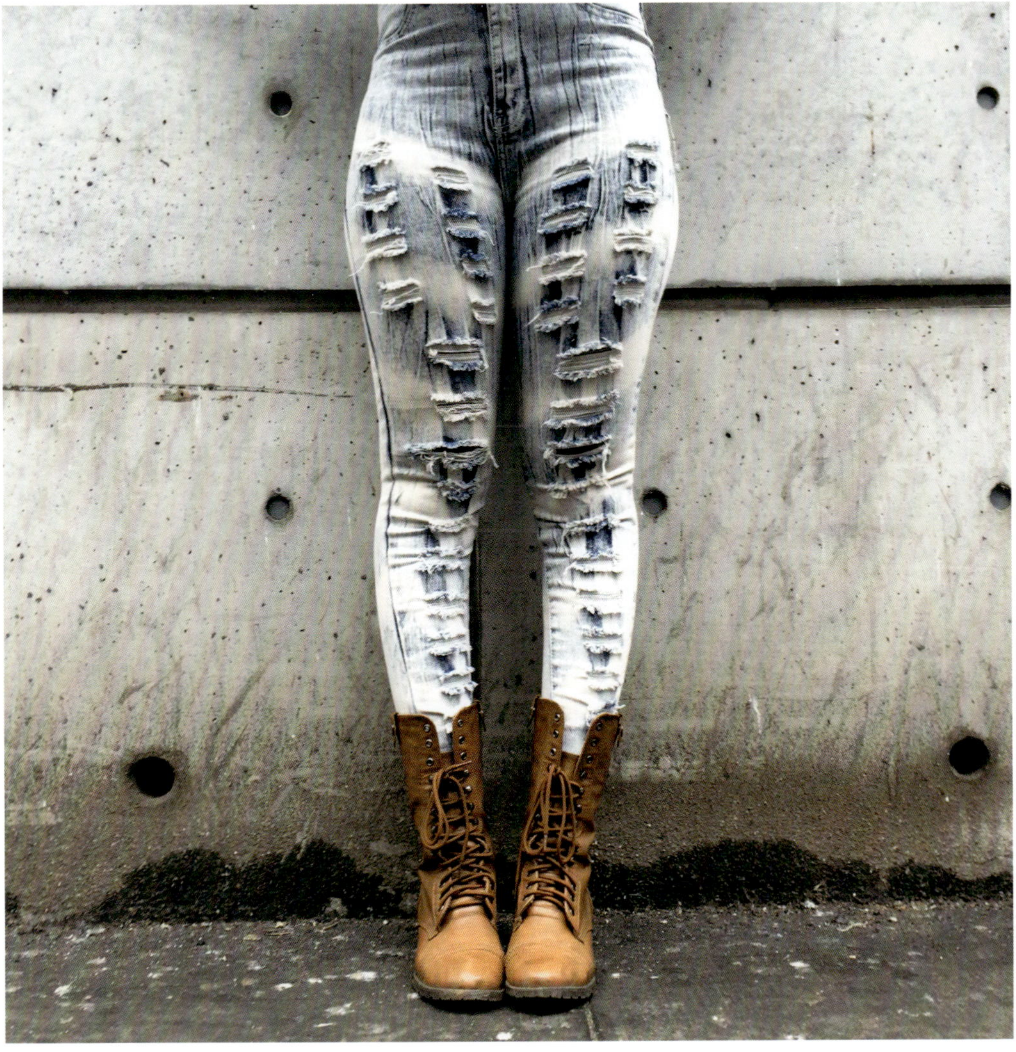

40th St., between 7th & 8th Aves.

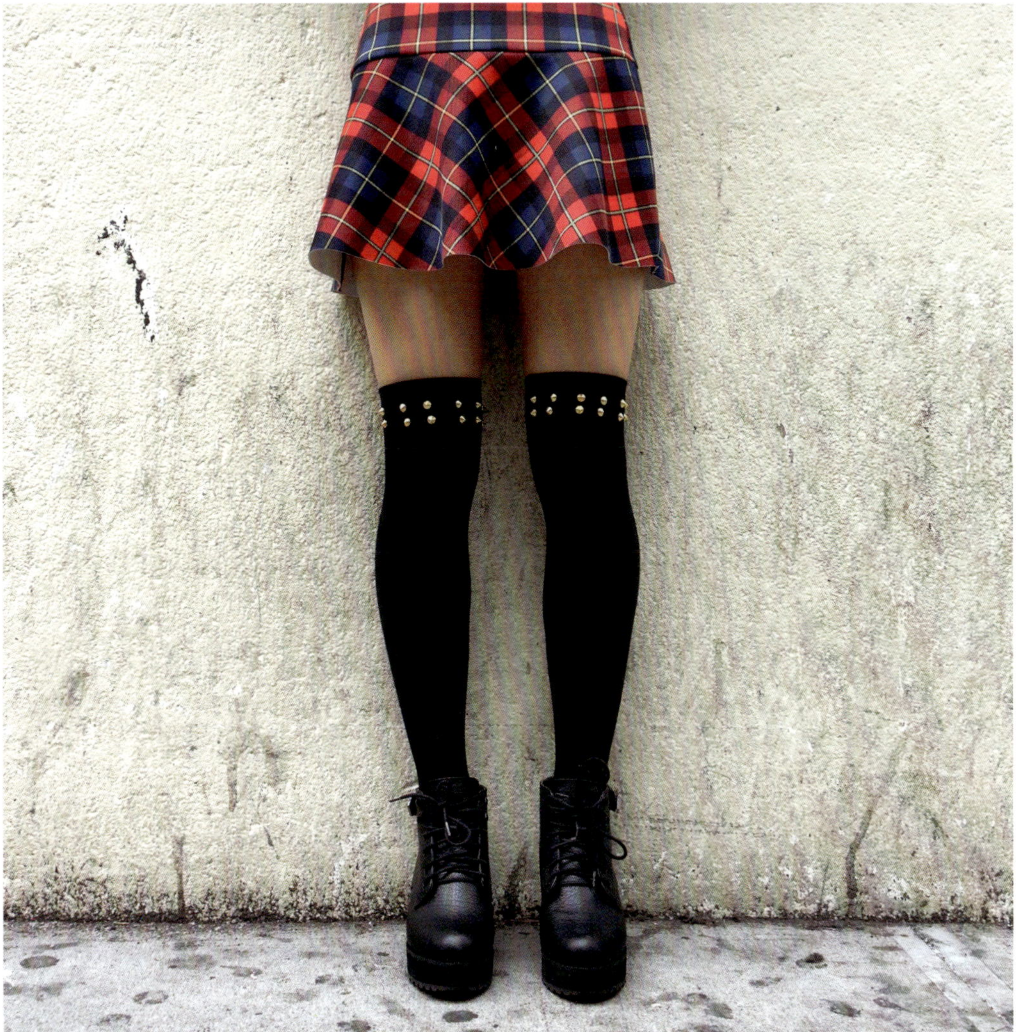

6th Ave., near West 4th St.

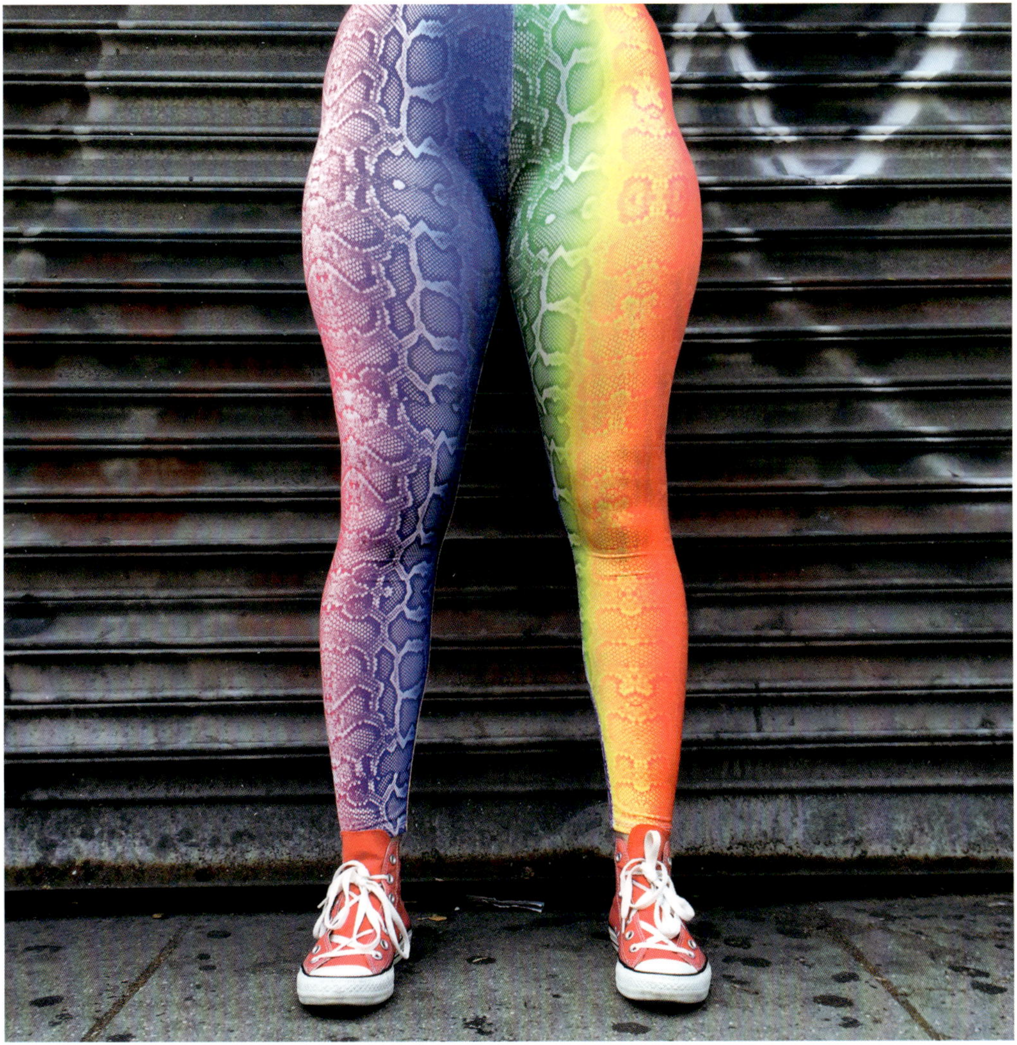

40th St., between 7th & 8th Aves.

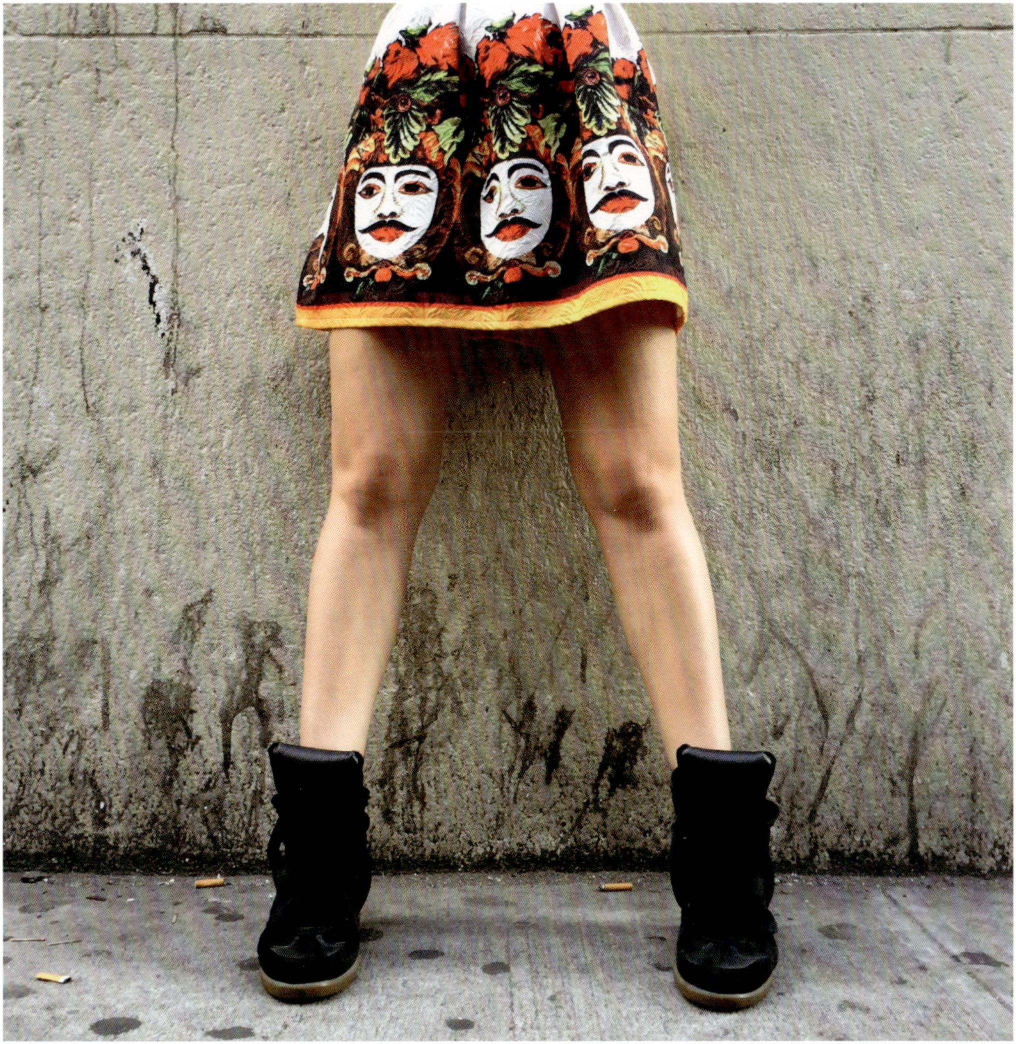

8th Ave., near 43rd St.

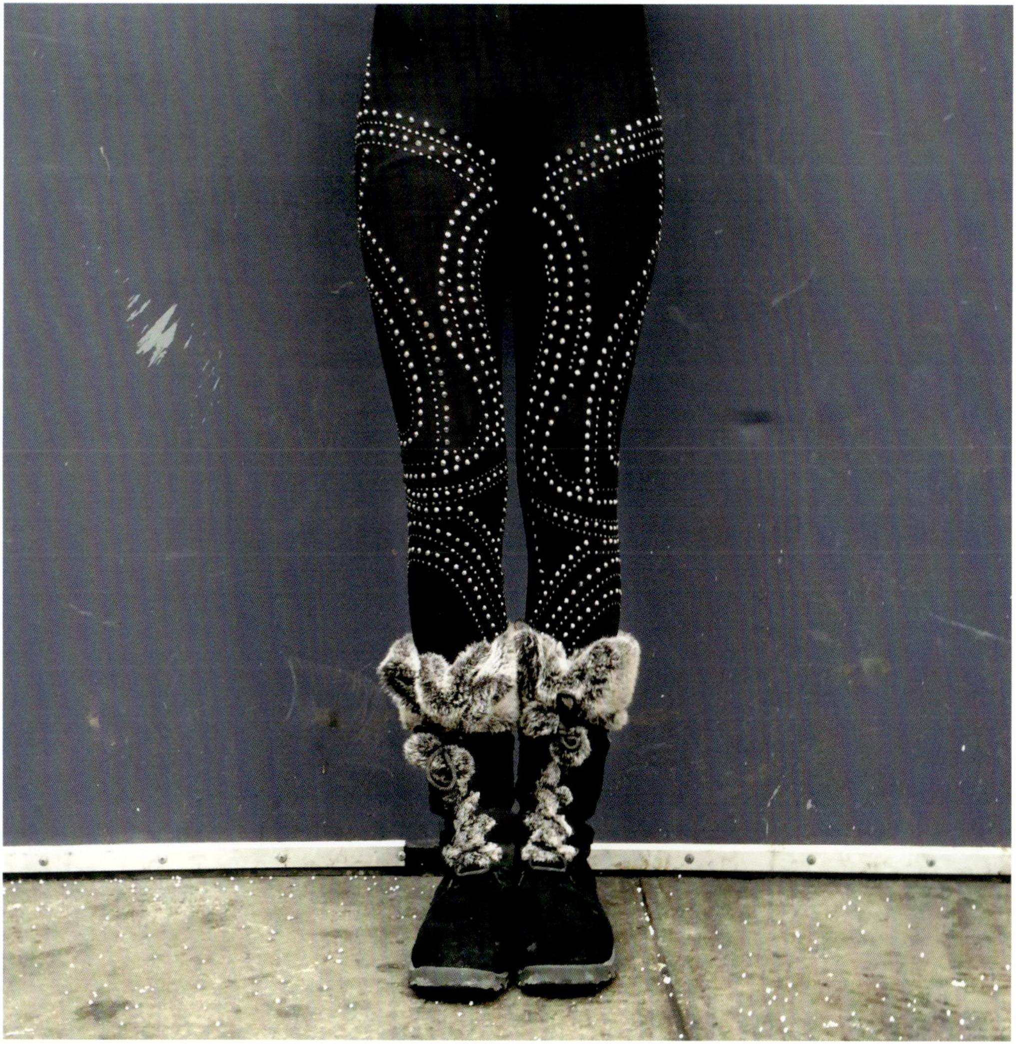

8th Ave., between 44th & 45th Sts.

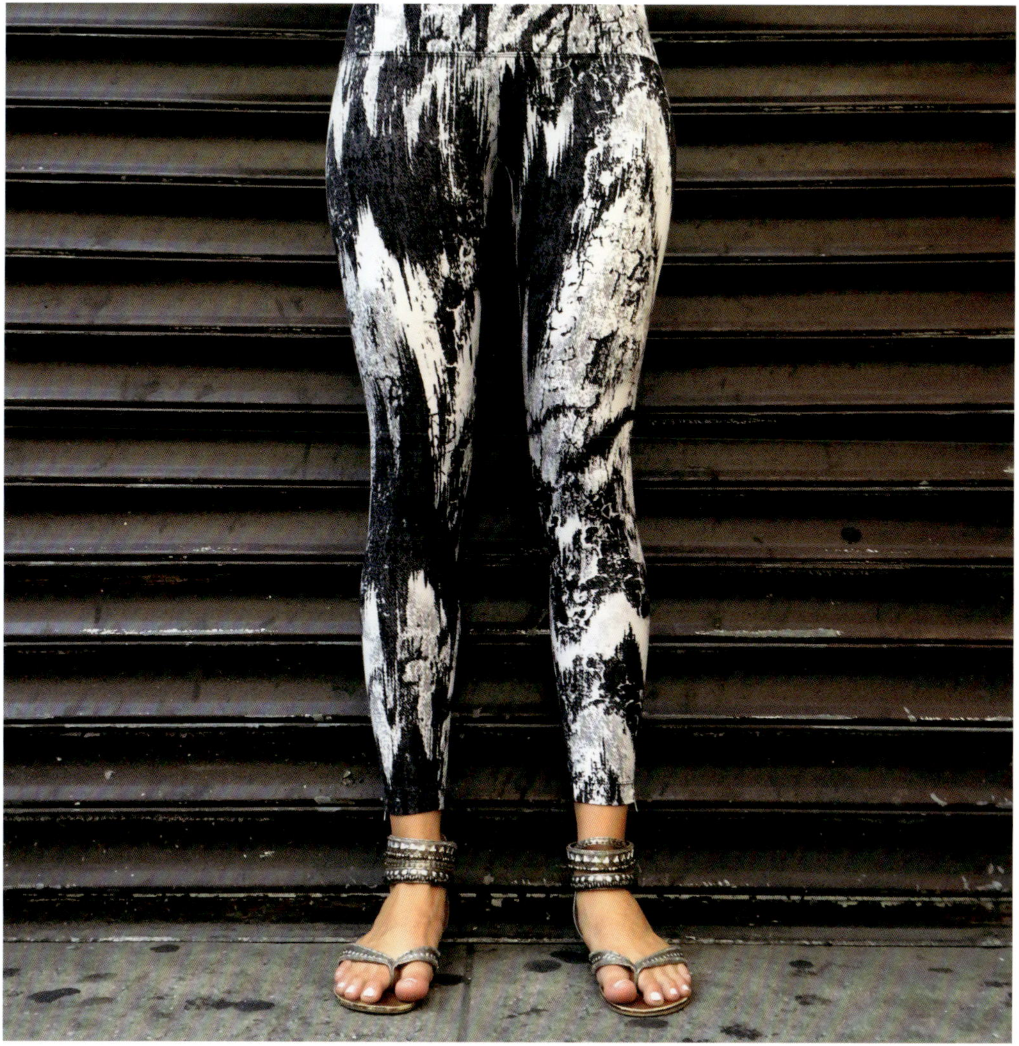

40th St., between 7th & 8th Aves.

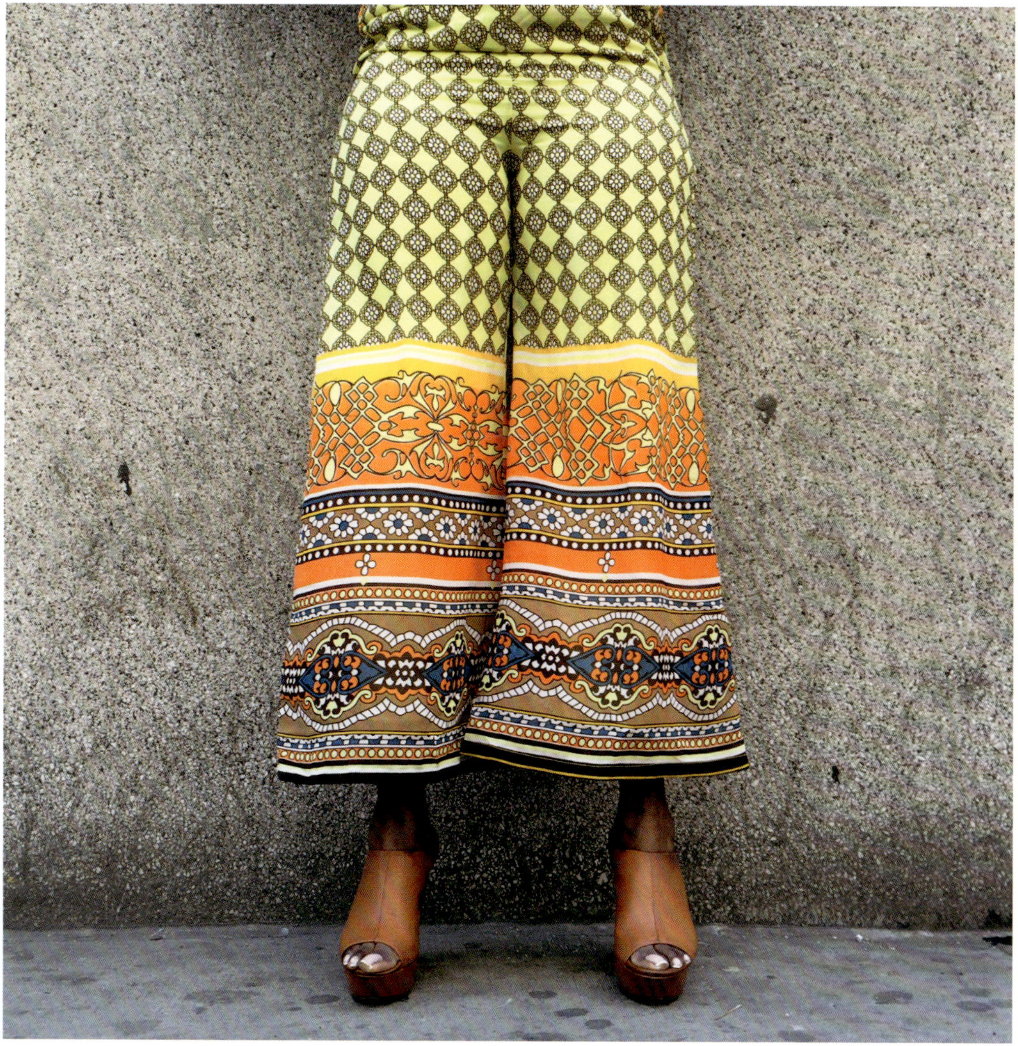

Elizabeth St., near Prince St.

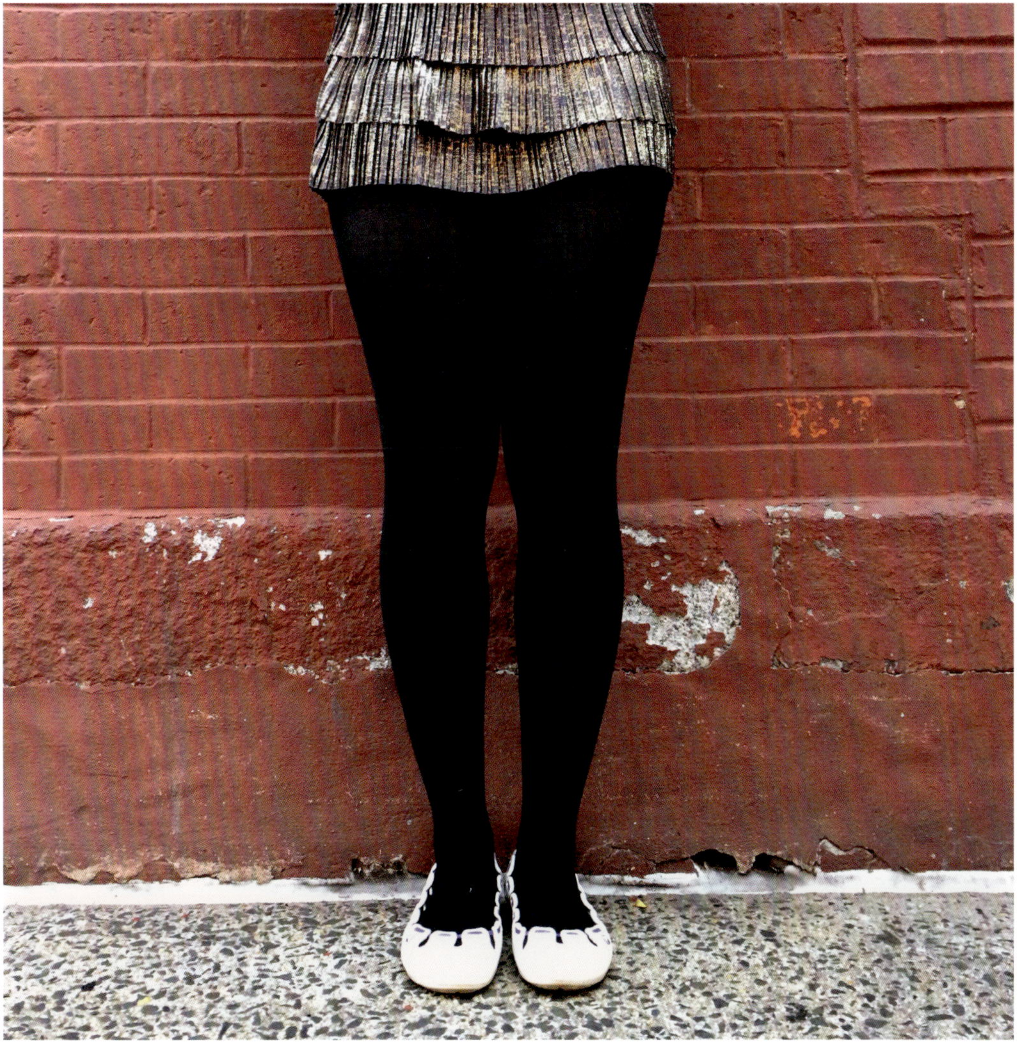

40th St., between 7th & 8th Aves.

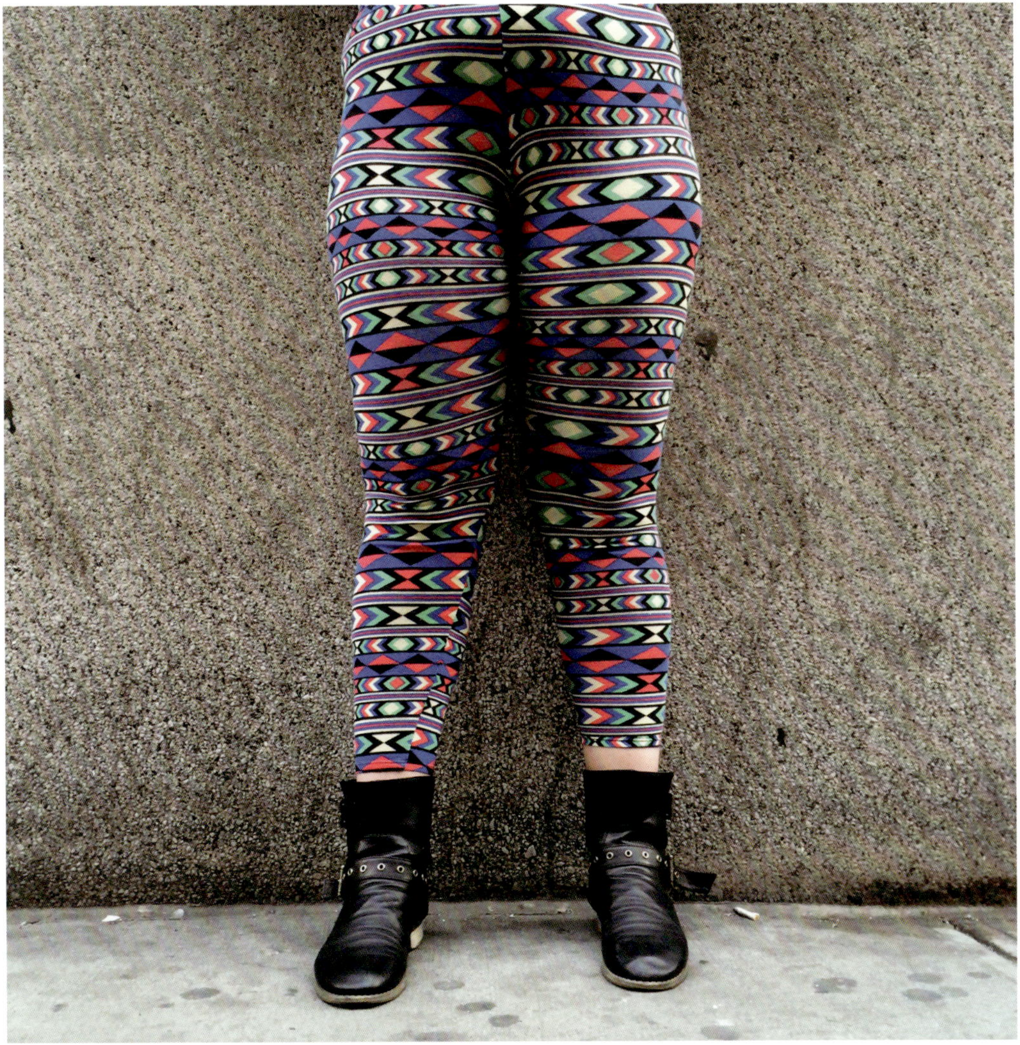

85th St. & Madison Ave.

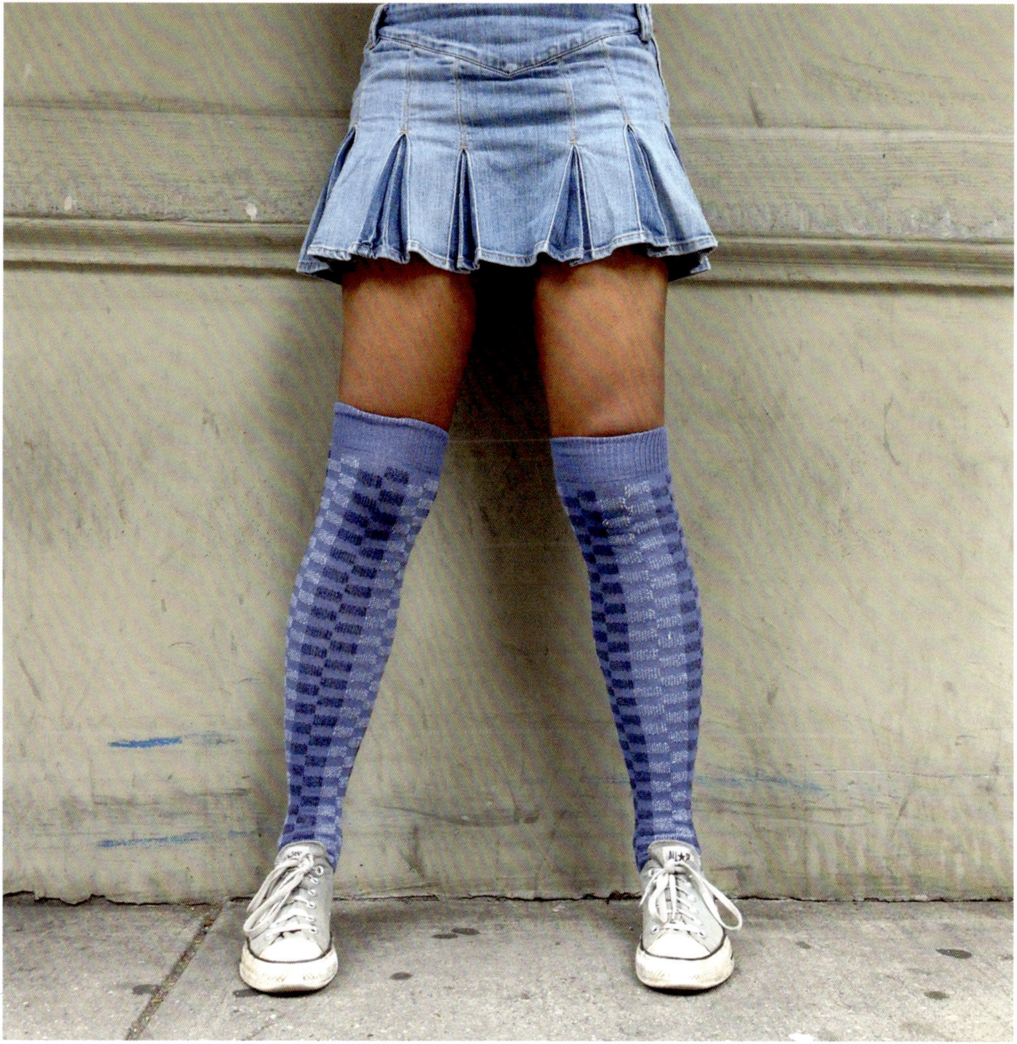

East Houston, near Broadway.

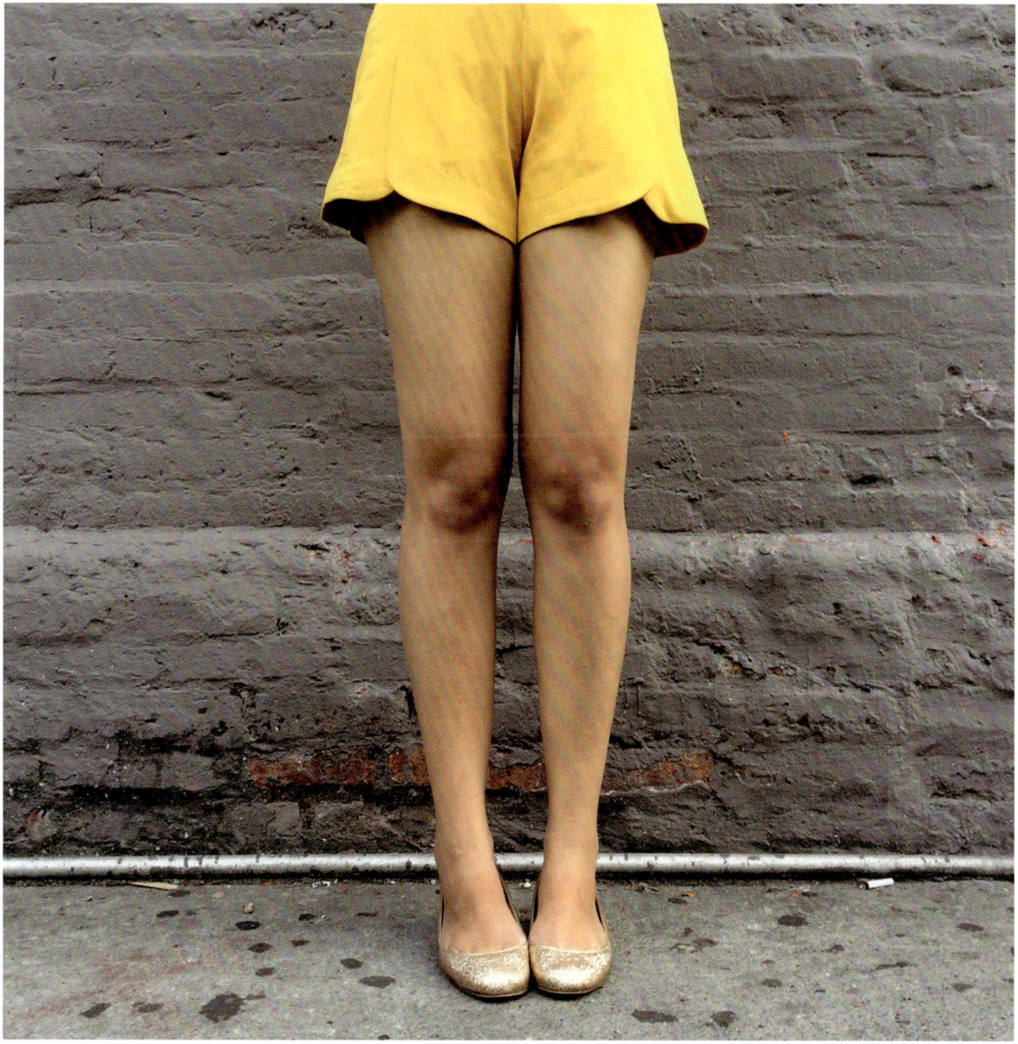

40th St., between 7th & 8th Aves.

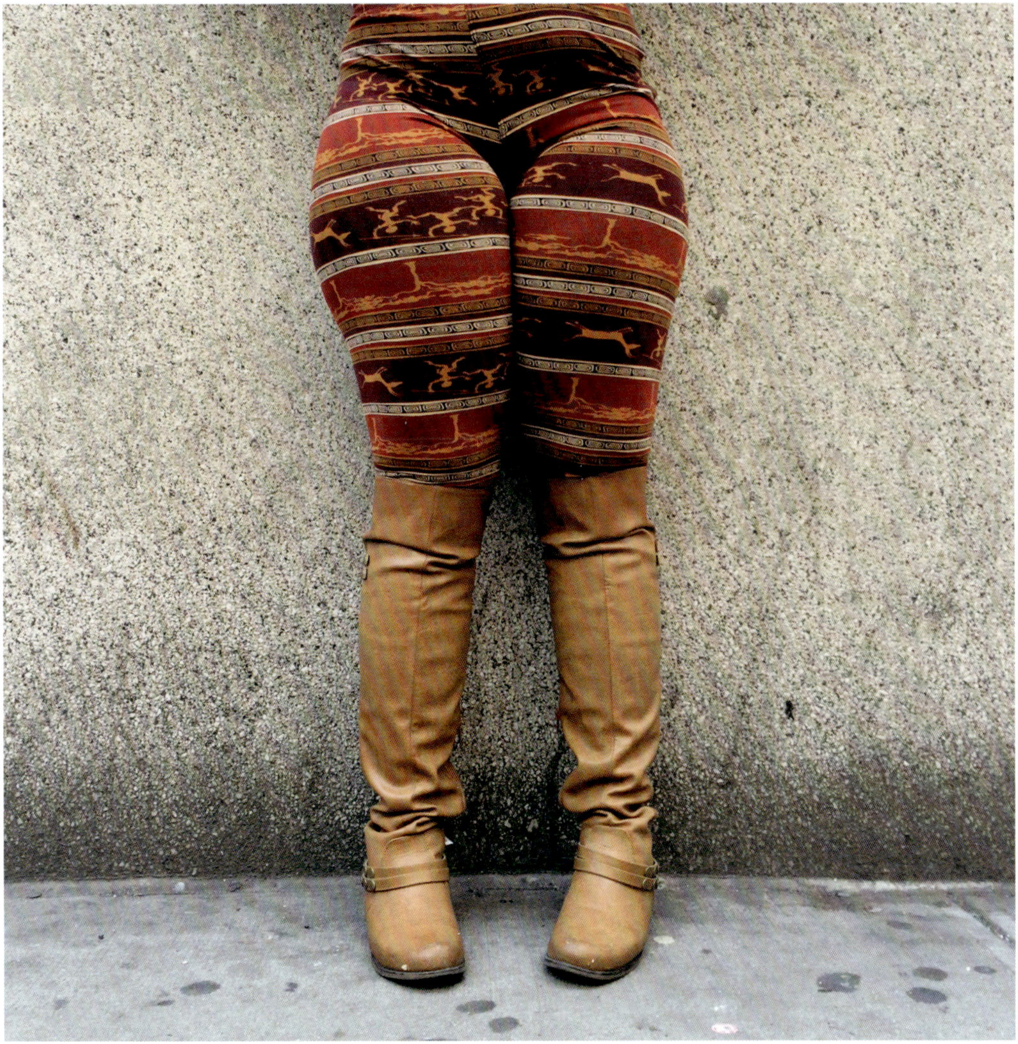

Mott & Prince Sts.

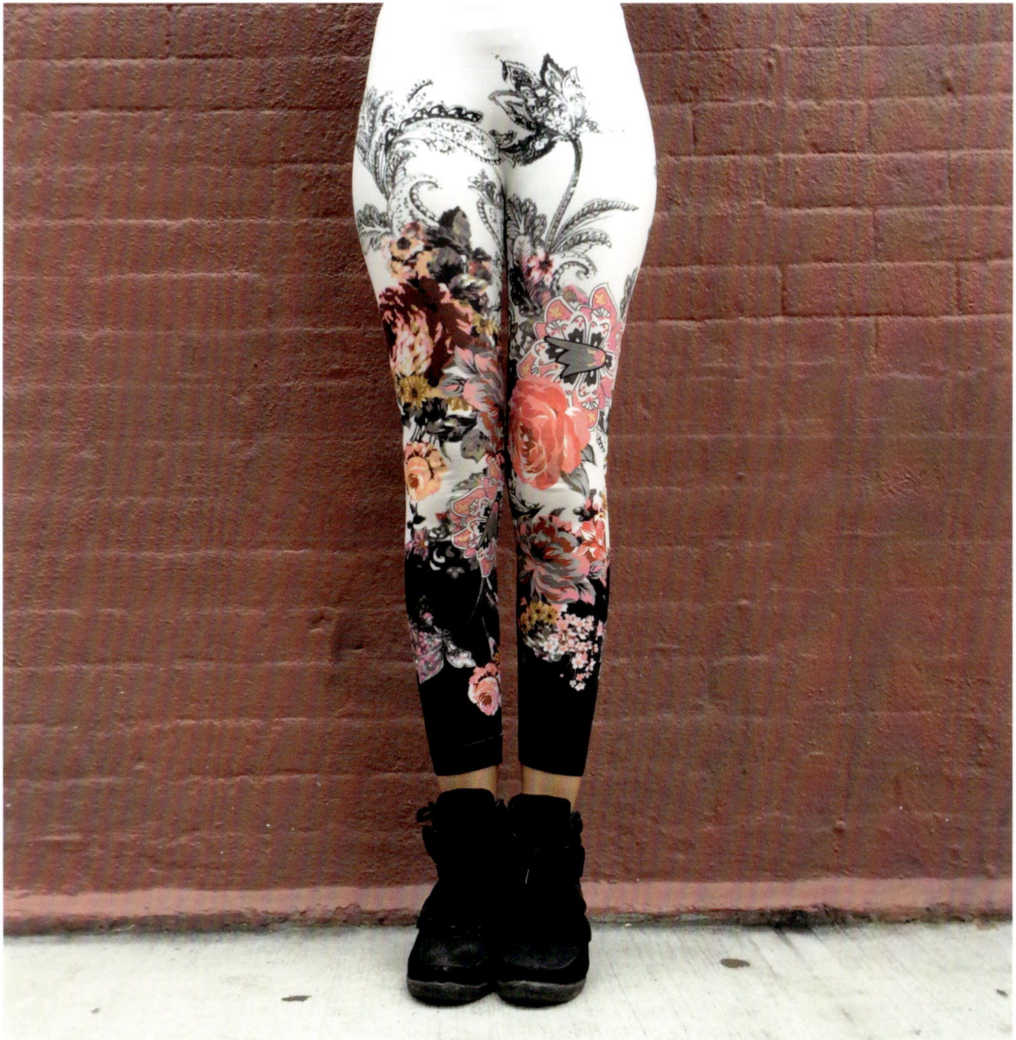

16th St., near 5th Ave.

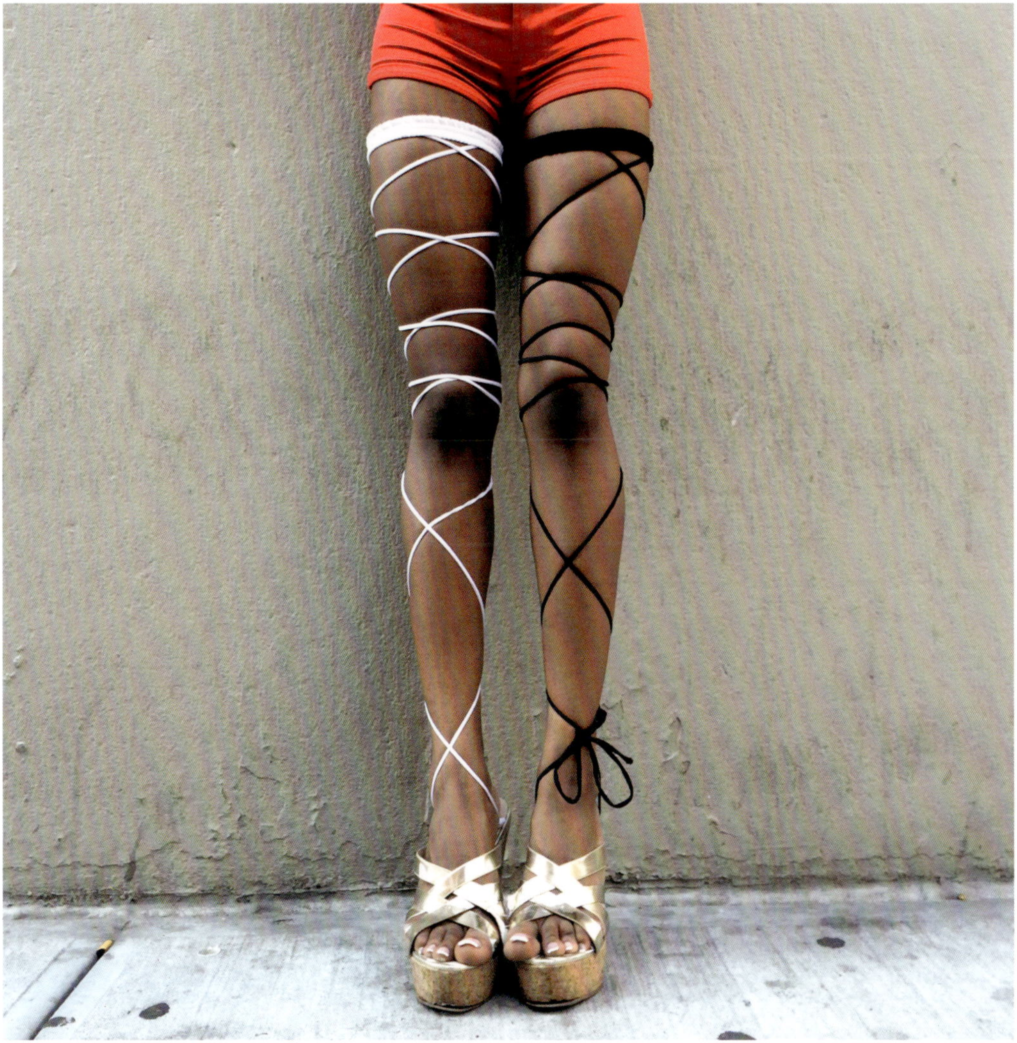

40th St., between 7th & 8th Aves.

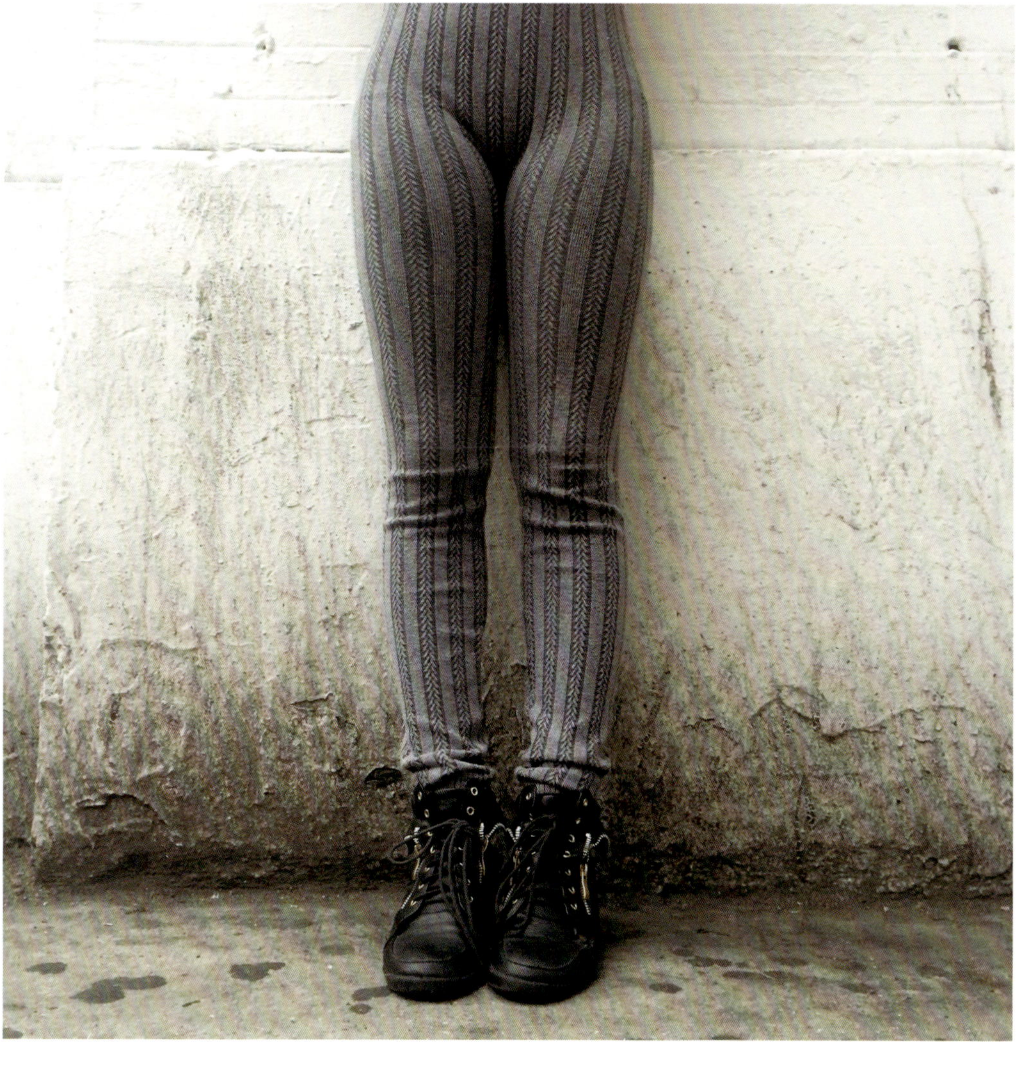

40th St., near 8th Ave.

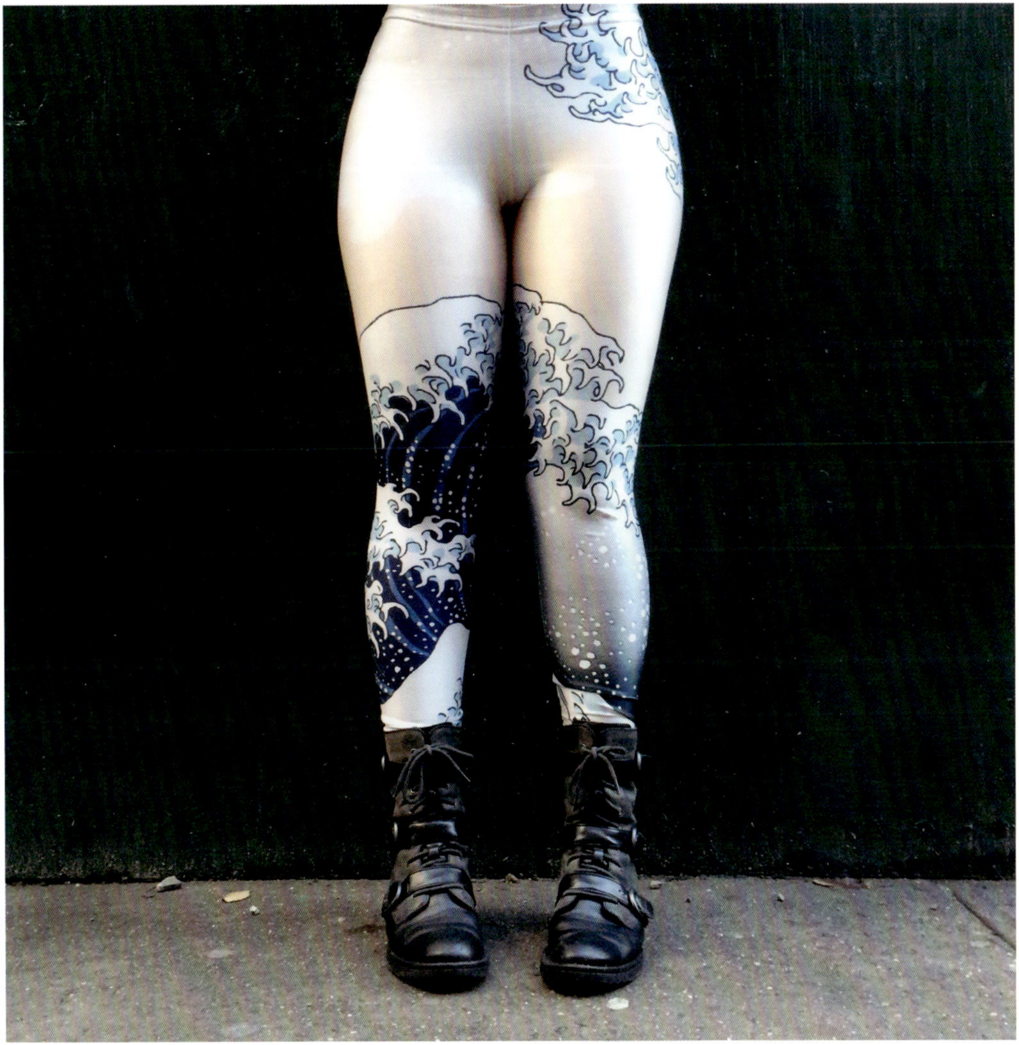

45th St. & 8th Ave.

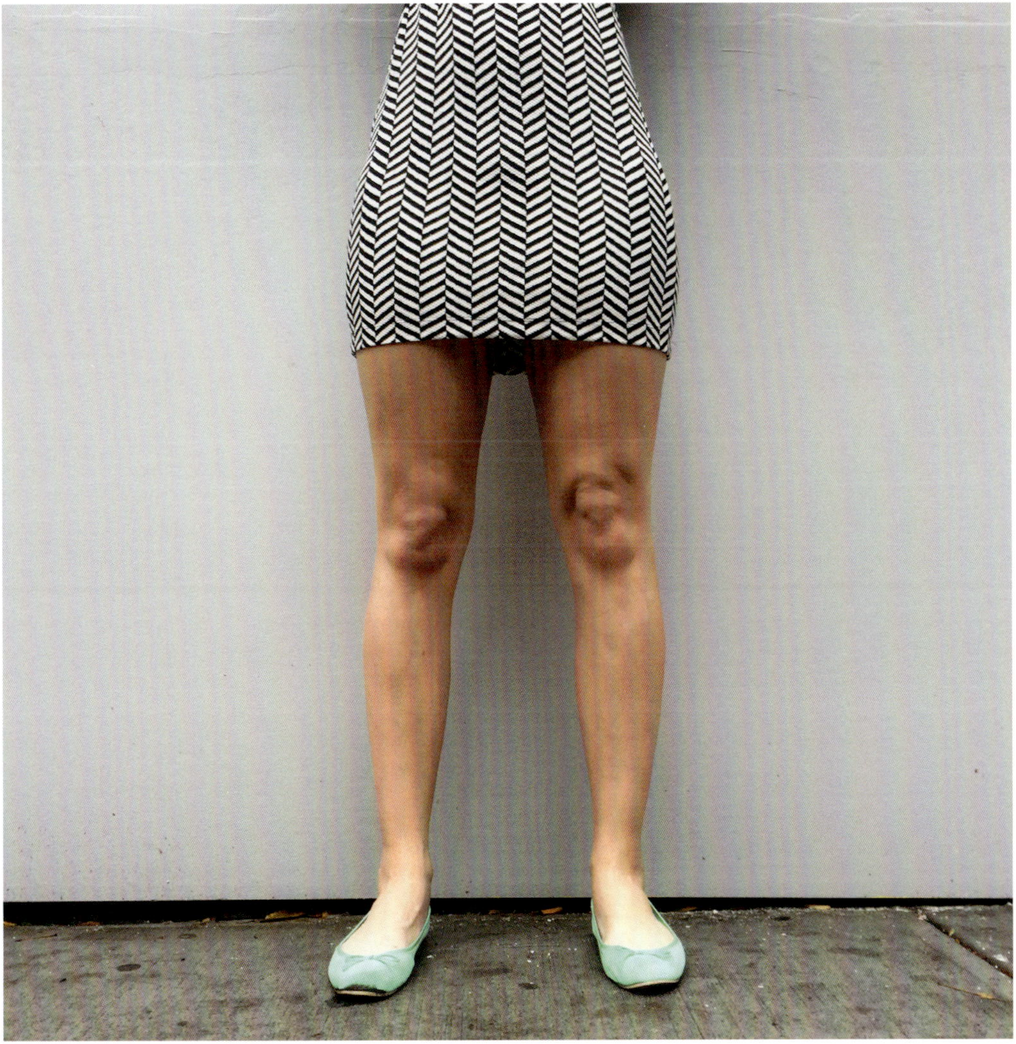

40th St., between 7th & 8th Aves.

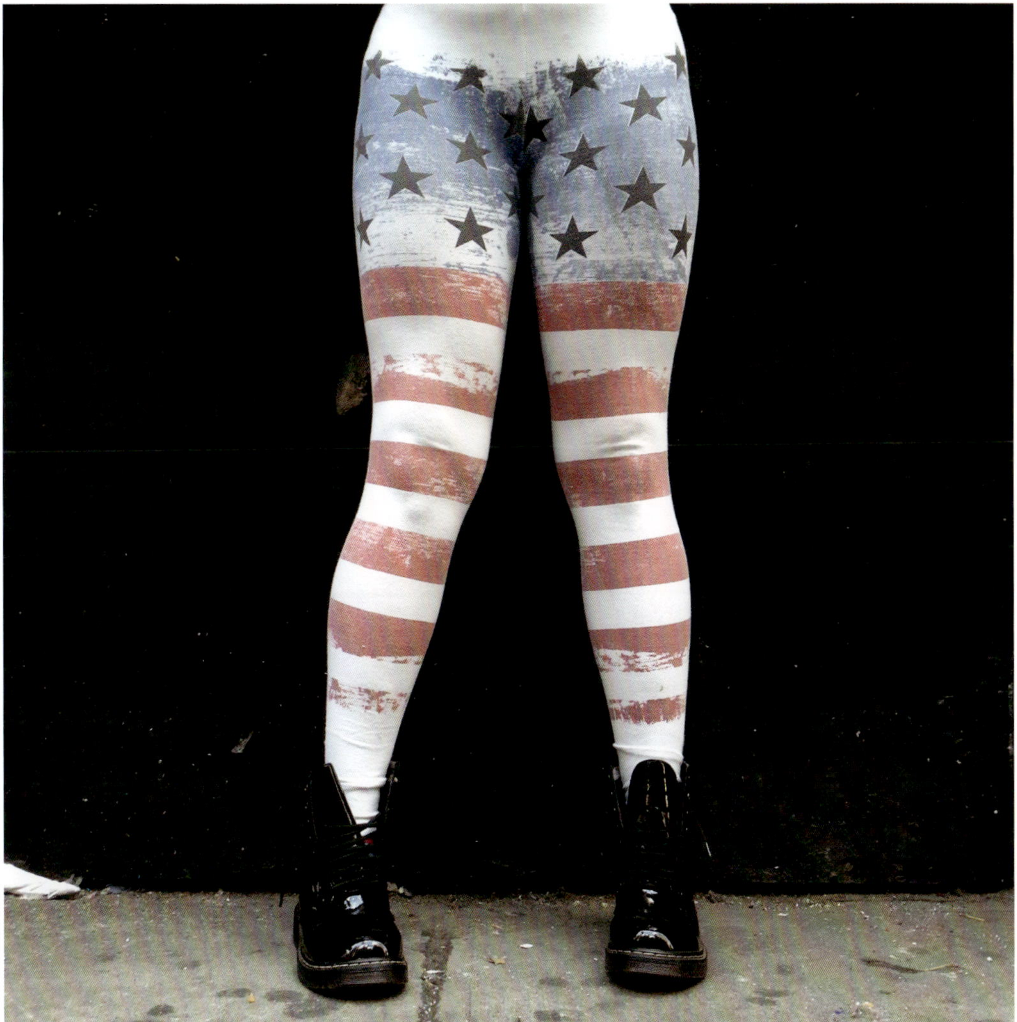

Houston & Lafayette Sts.

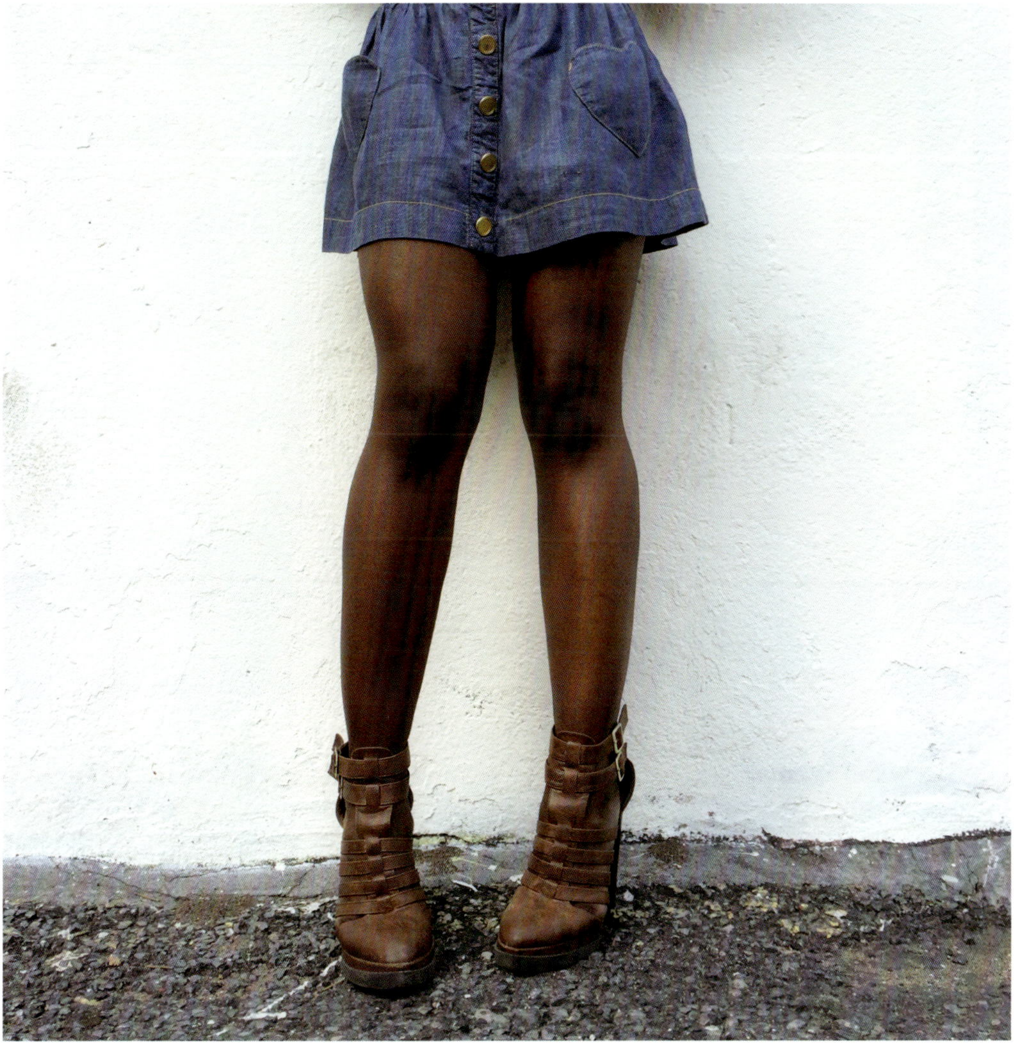

125th St., near Lexington Ave.

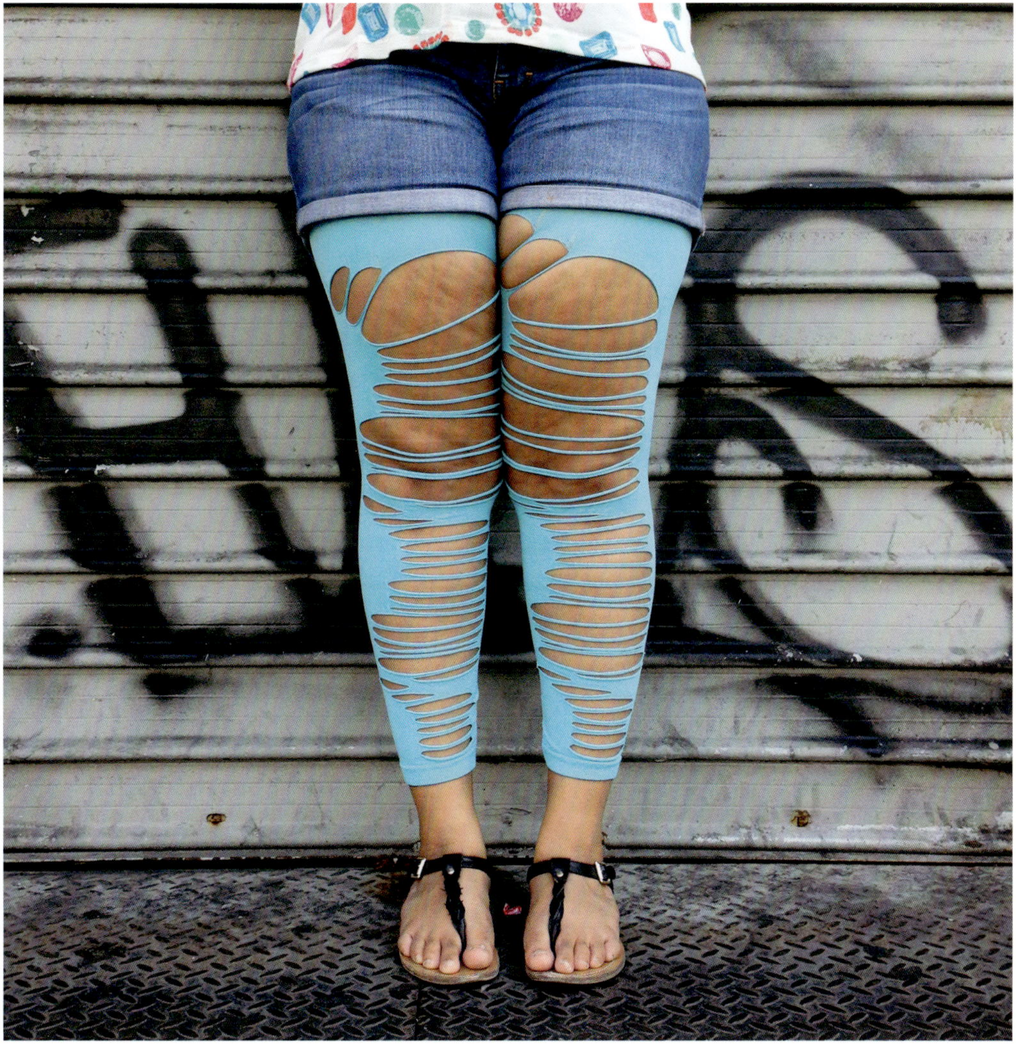

Madison Ave., near 125th St.

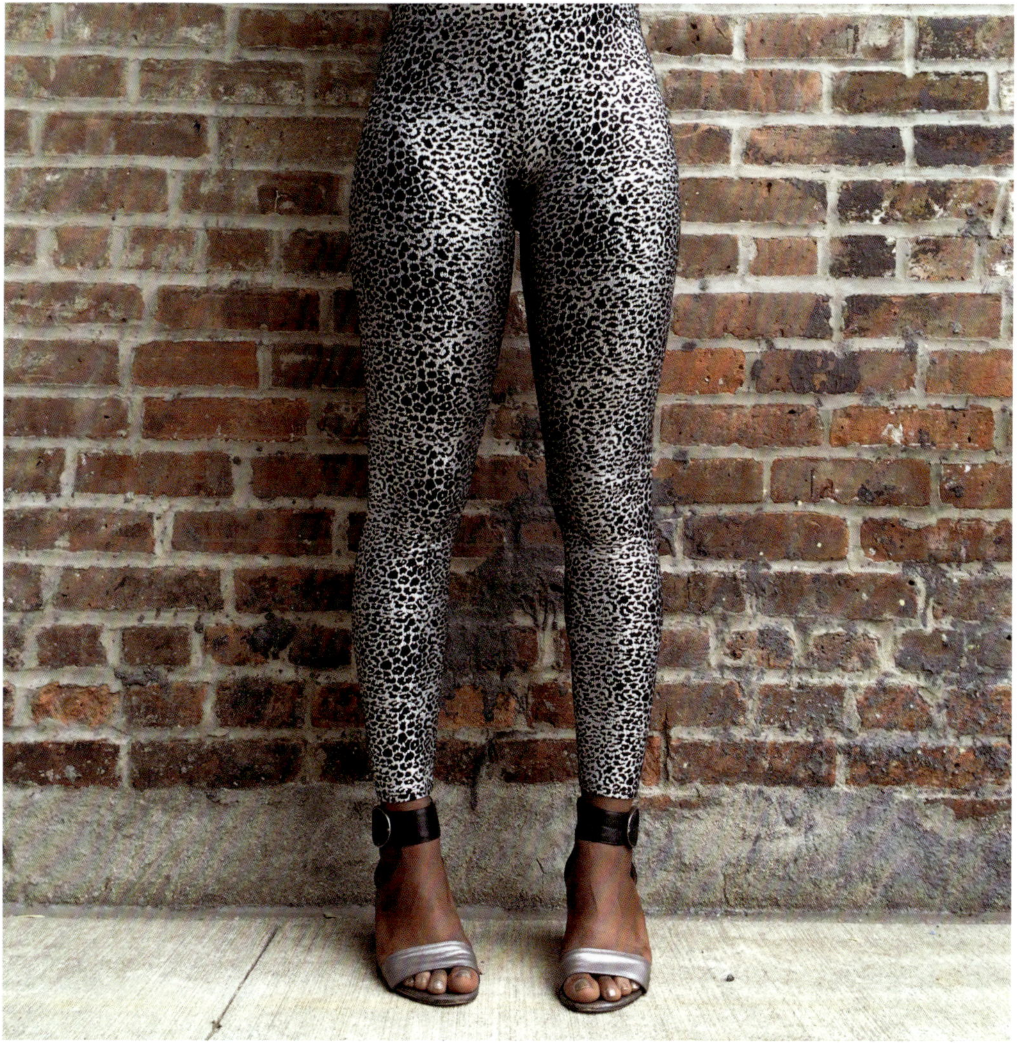

Prince & Mott Sts.

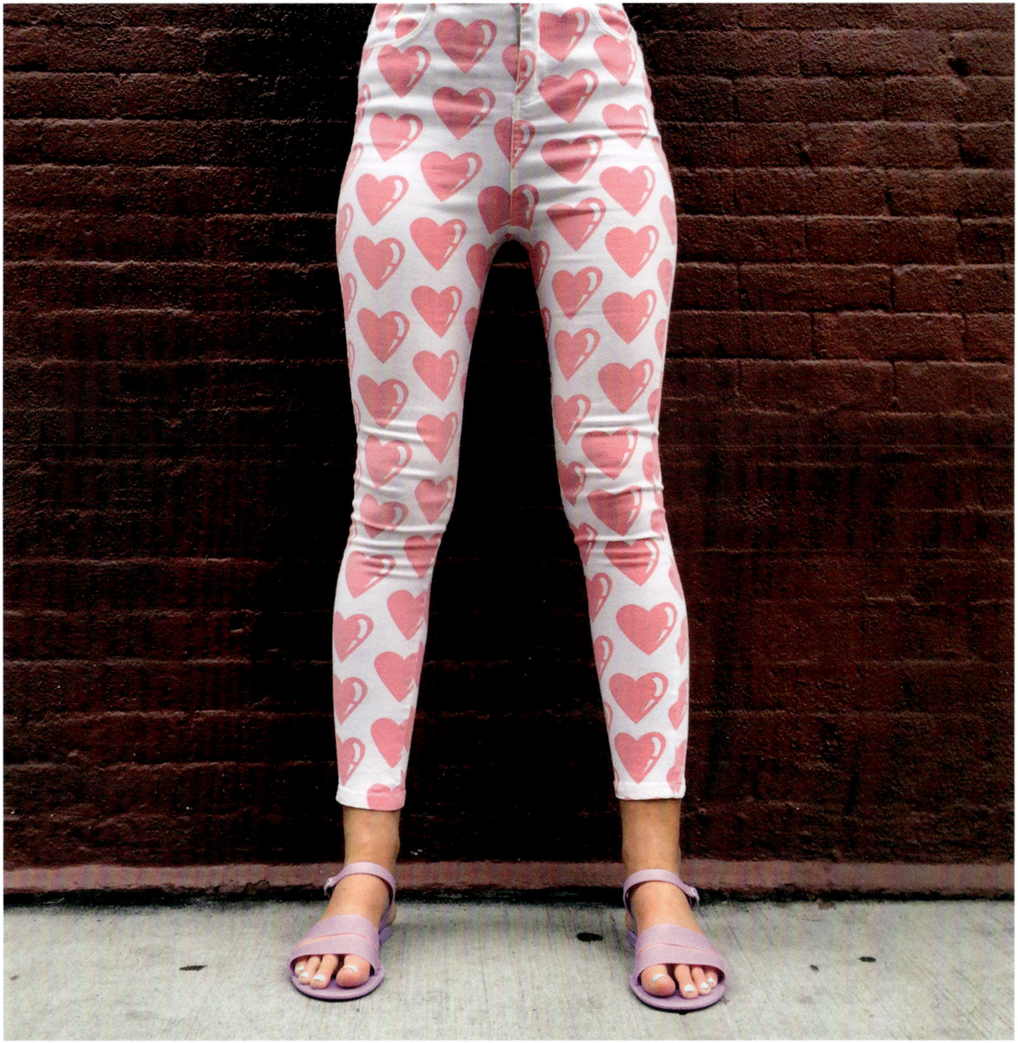

42nd St., near 5th Ave.

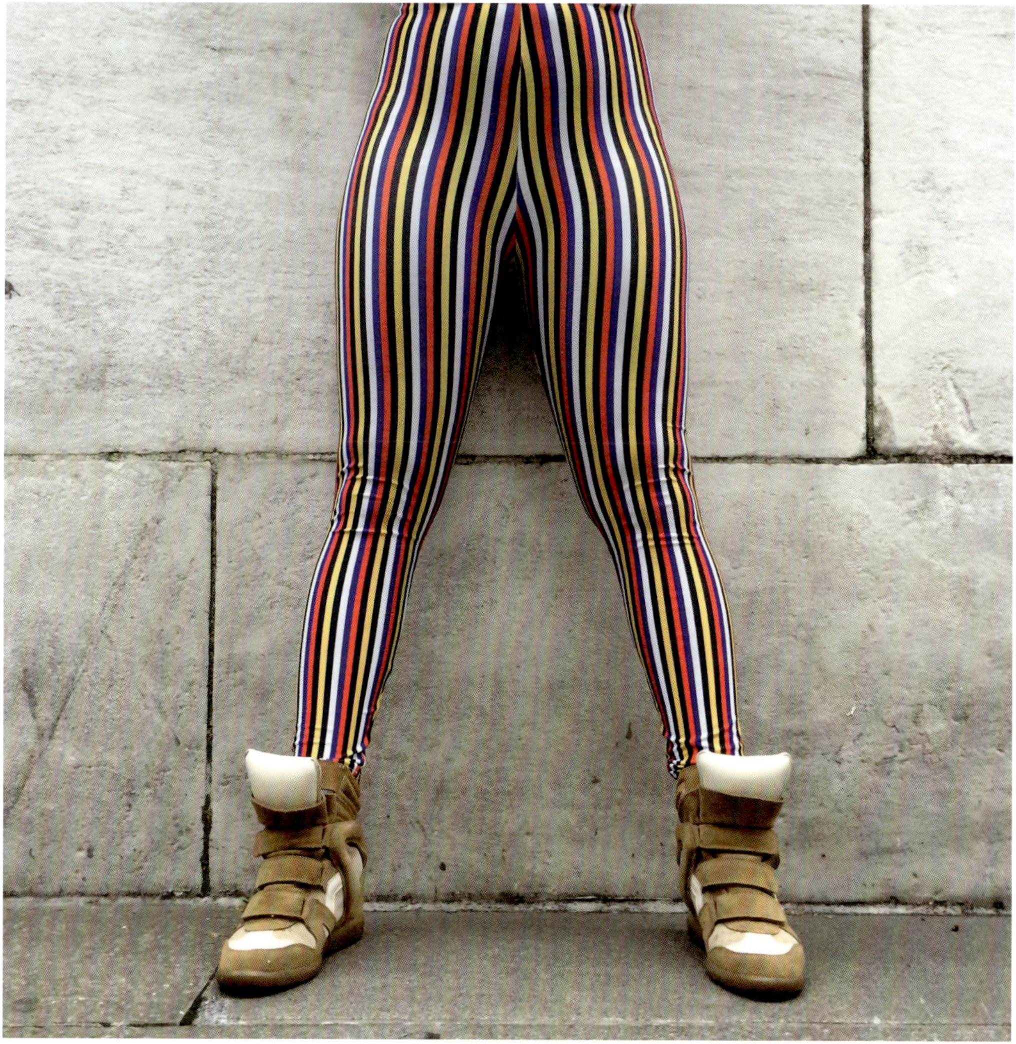

Columbus Ave. & 66th St.

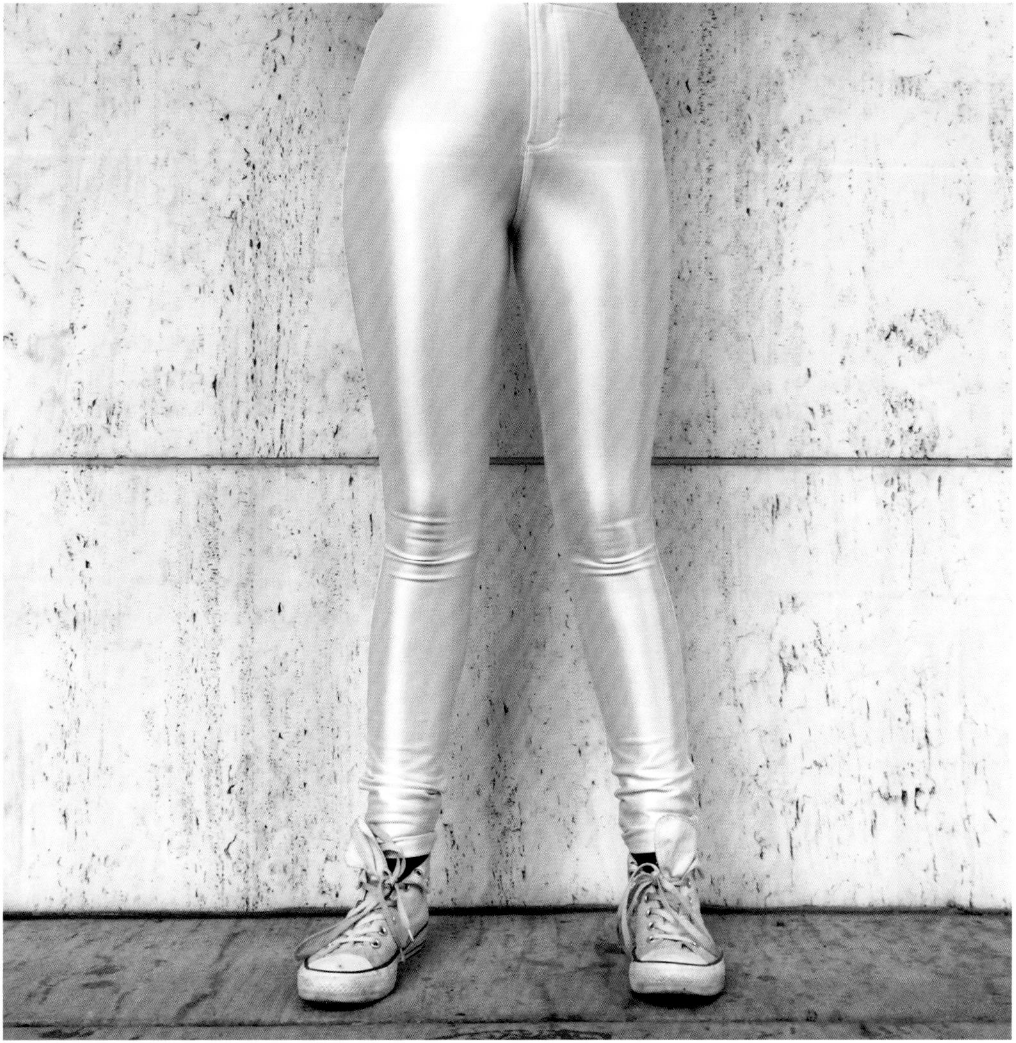

40th St., between 7th & 8th Aves.

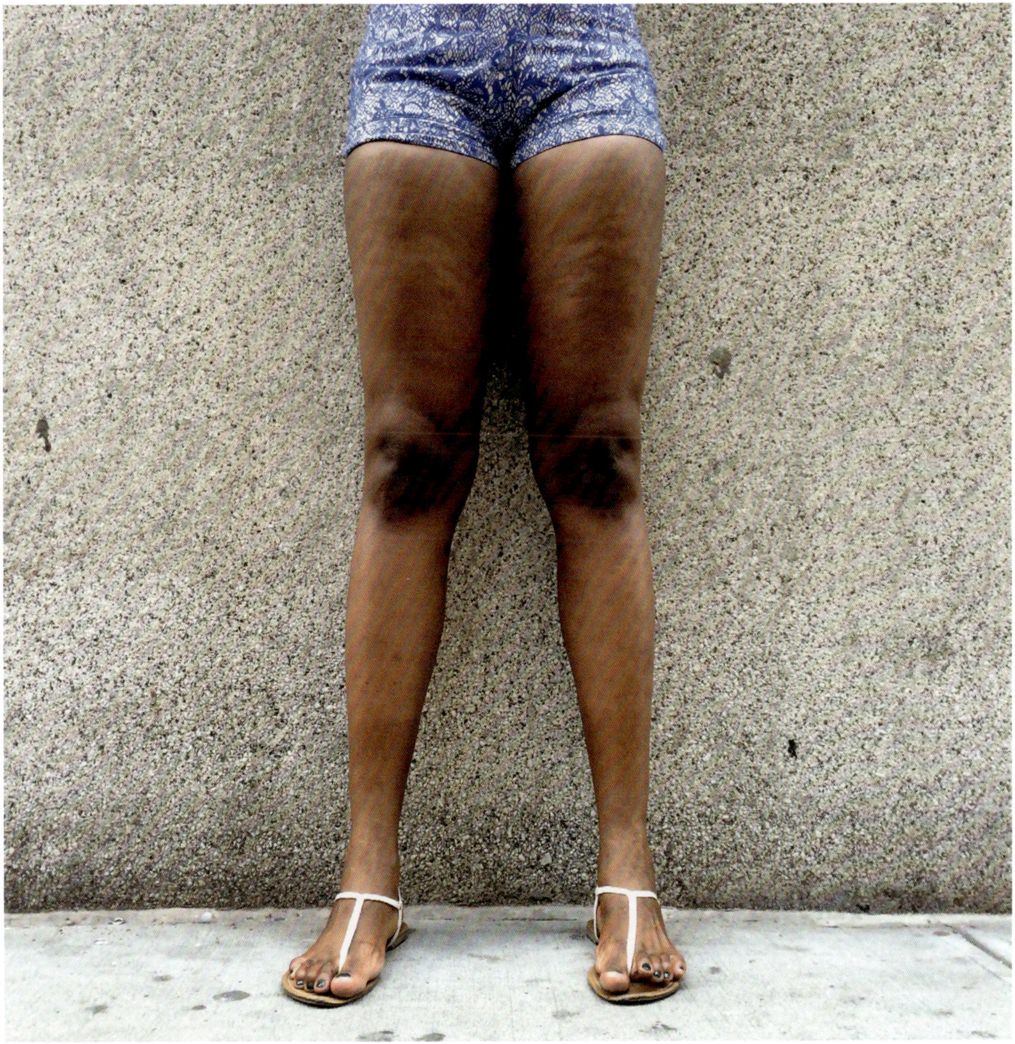

40th St., between 7th & 8th Aves.

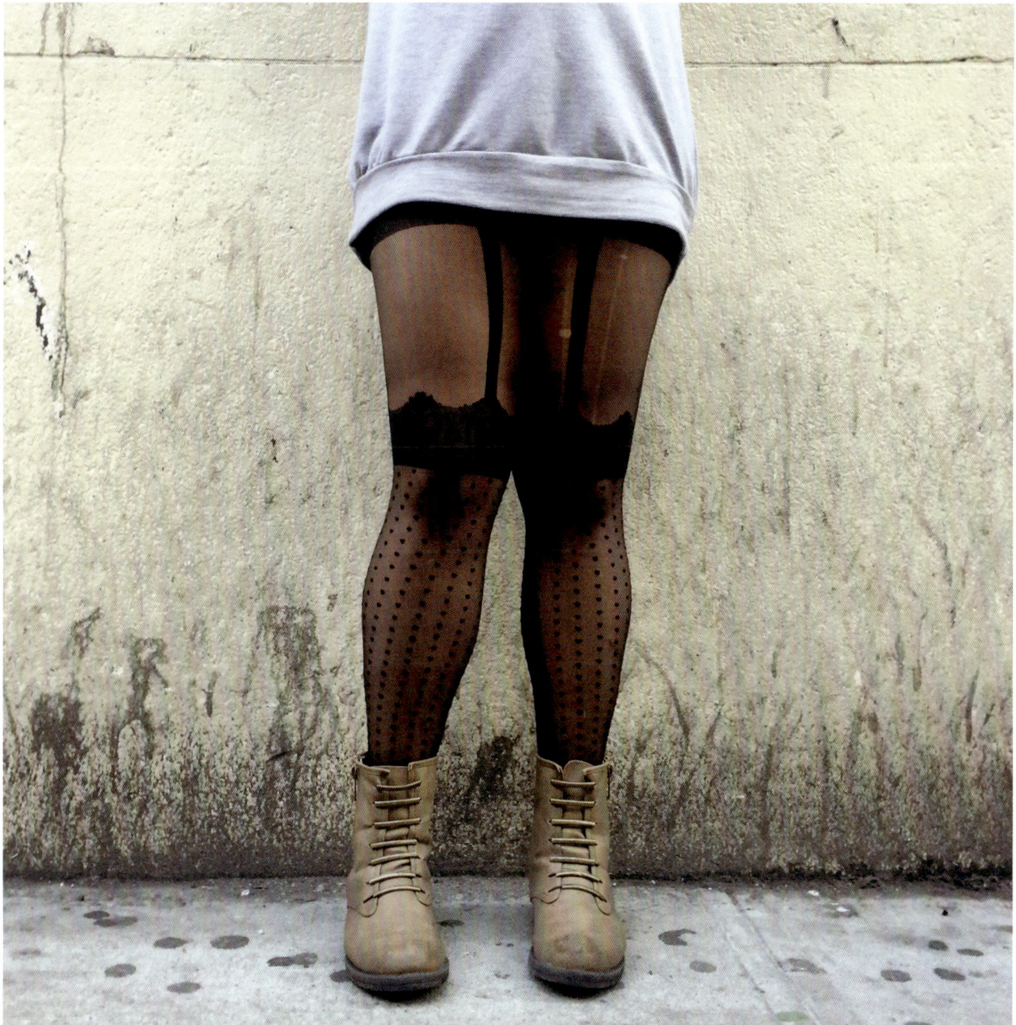

125th St. & Lexington Ave.

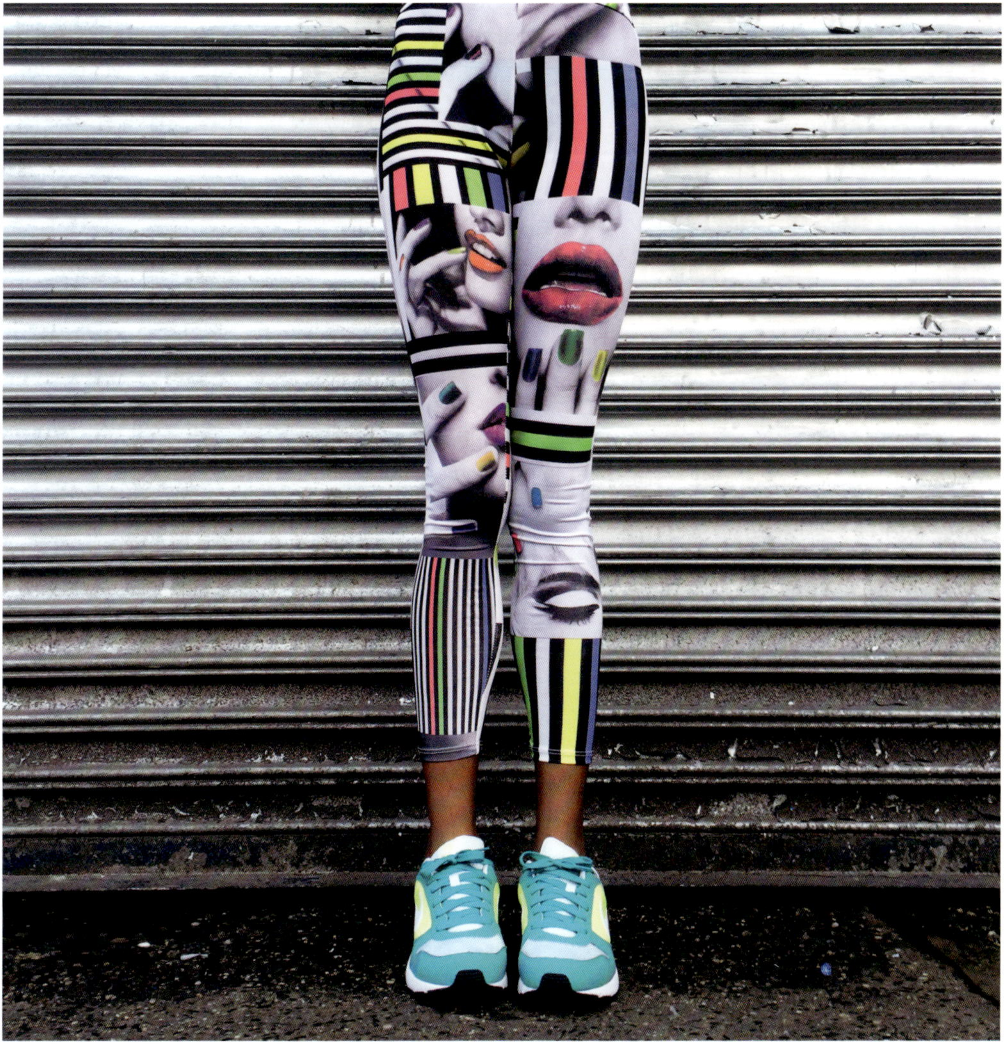

40th St., between 7th & 8th Aves.

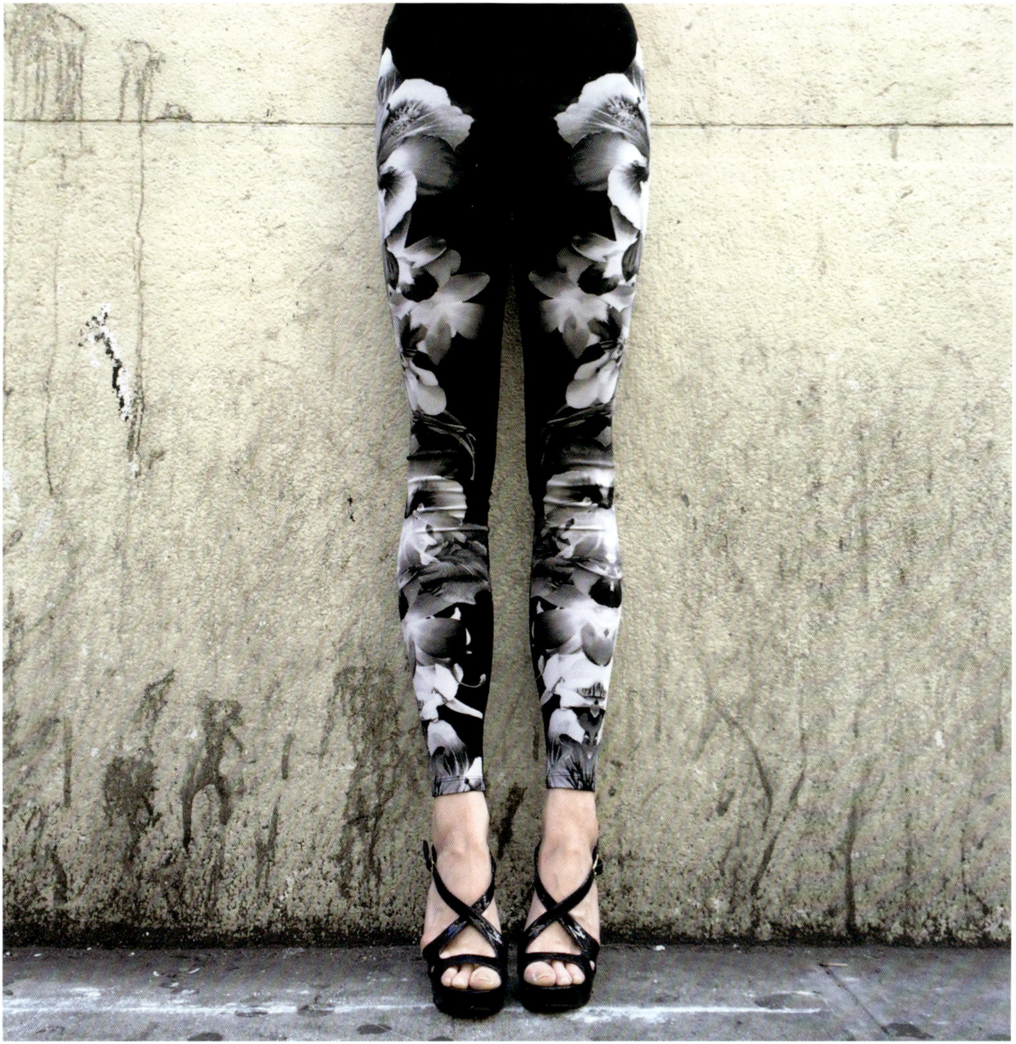

51st St., near 8th Ave.

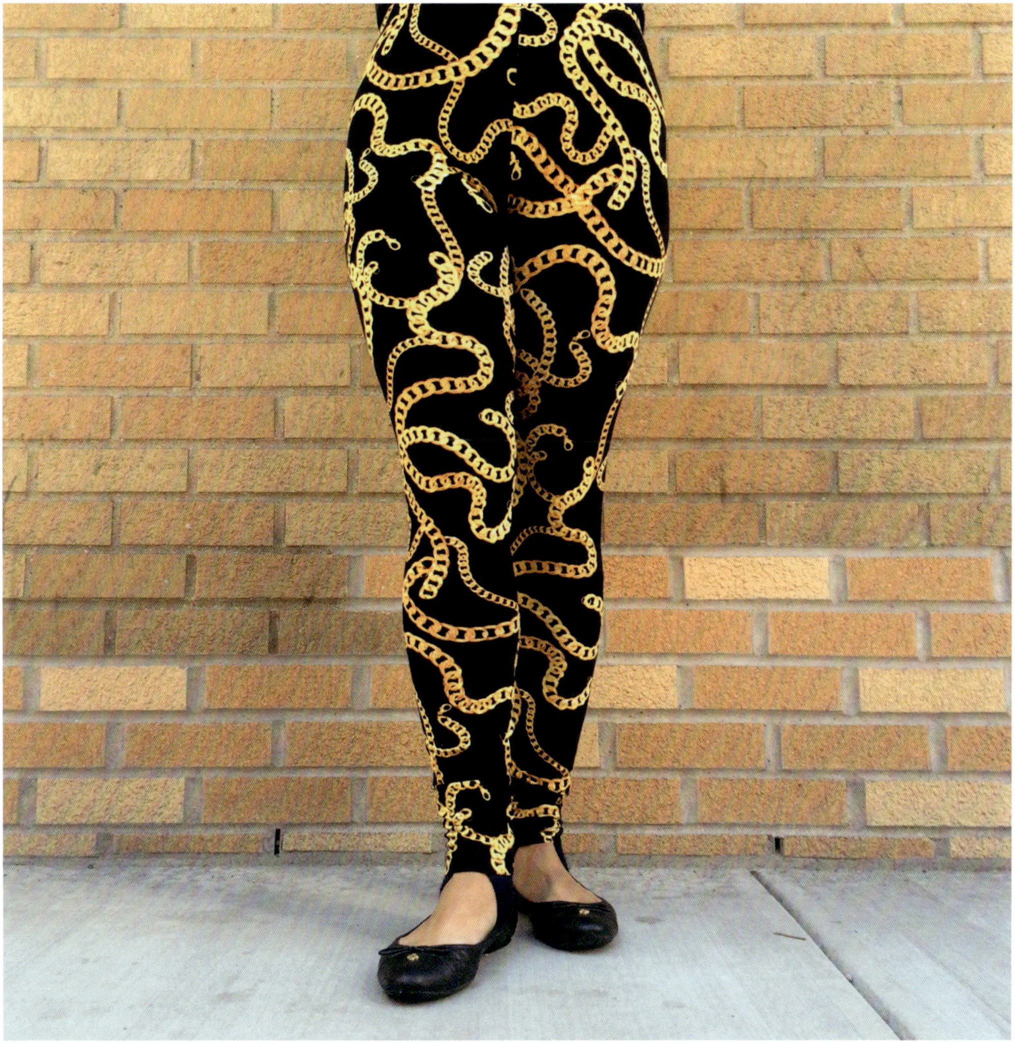

44th St., near 8th Ave.

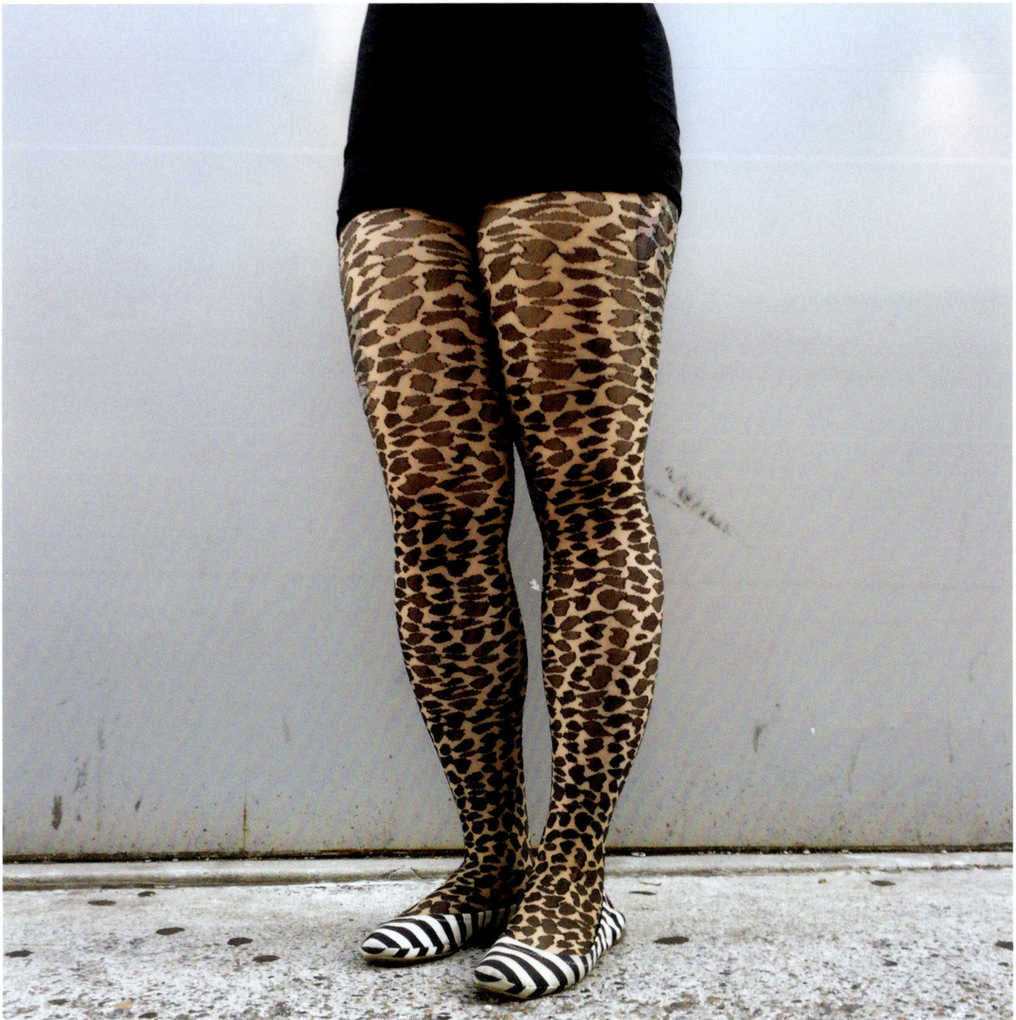

8th Ave., between 34th & 35th Sts.

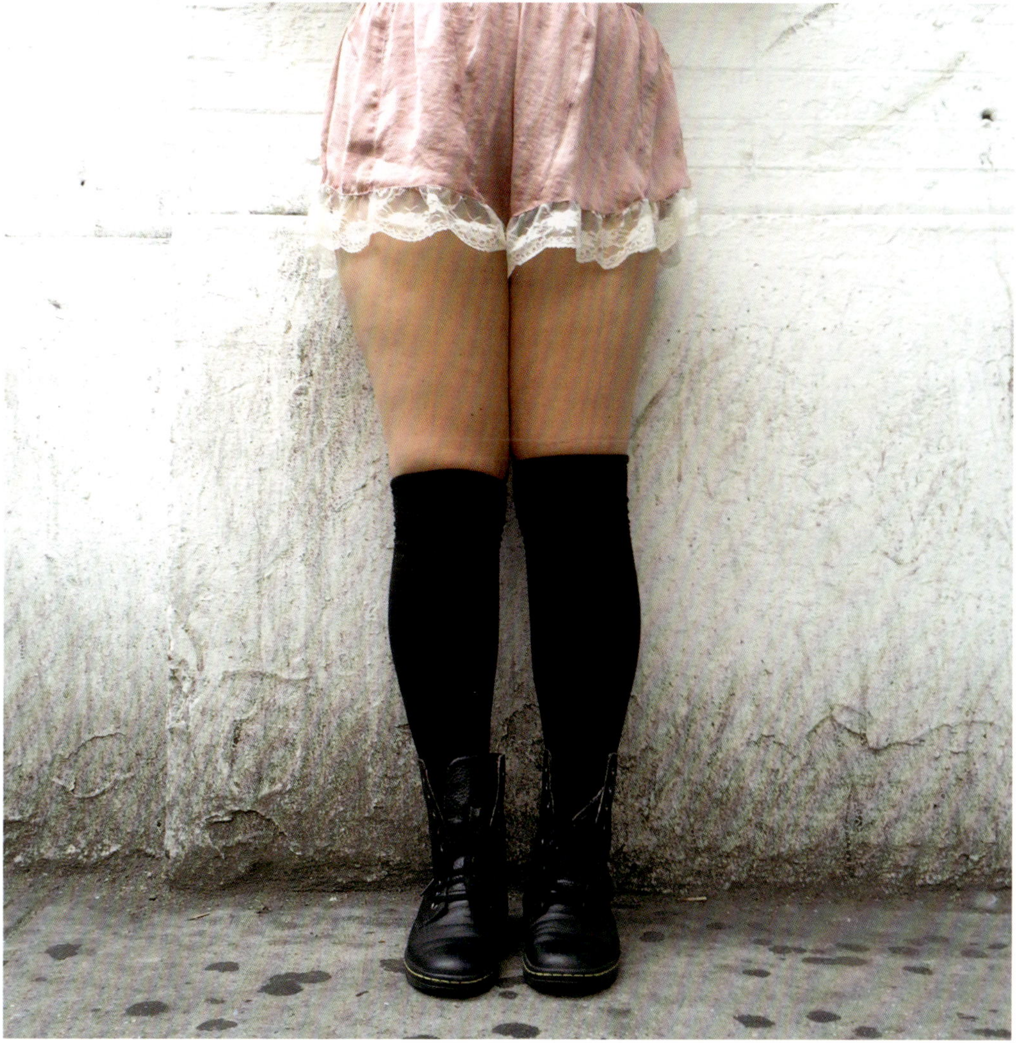

40th St., between 7th & 8th Aves.

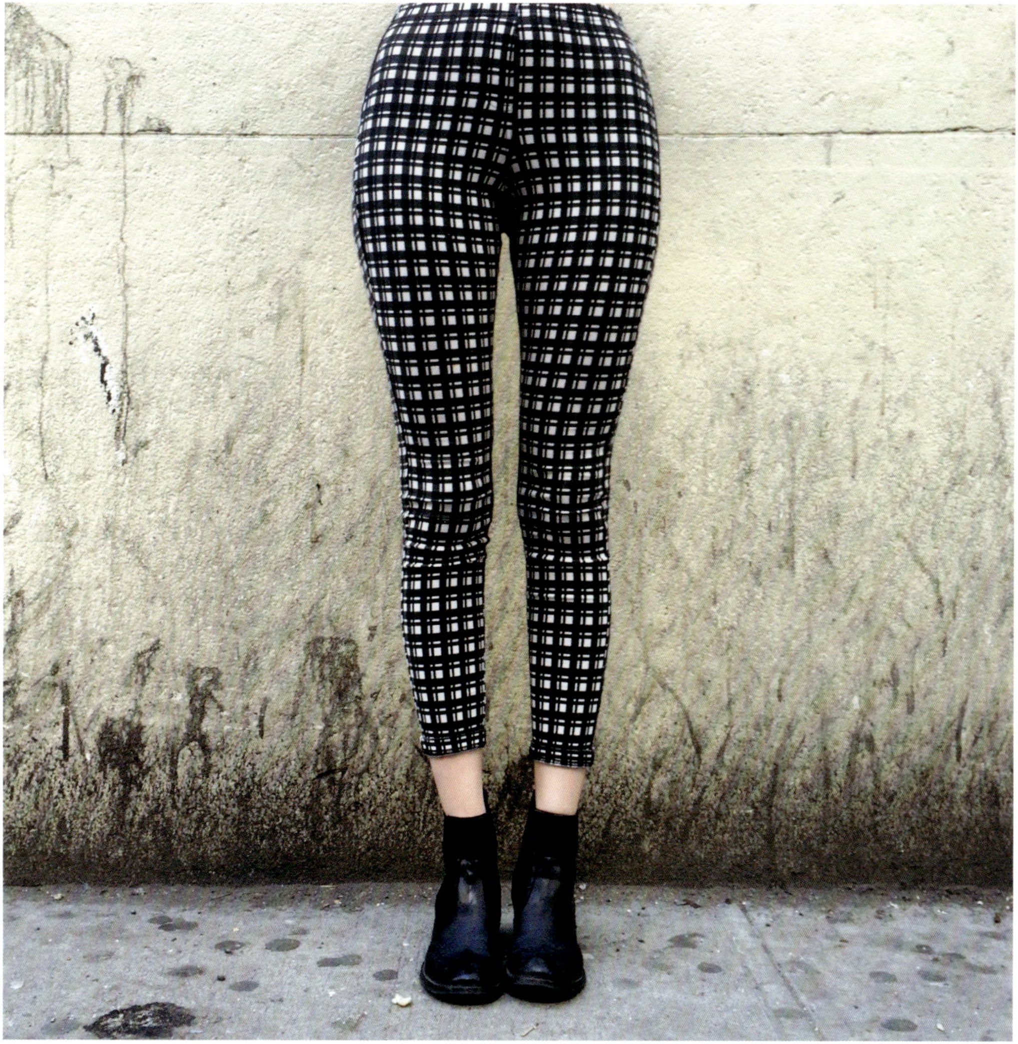

5th Ave. & 12th St.

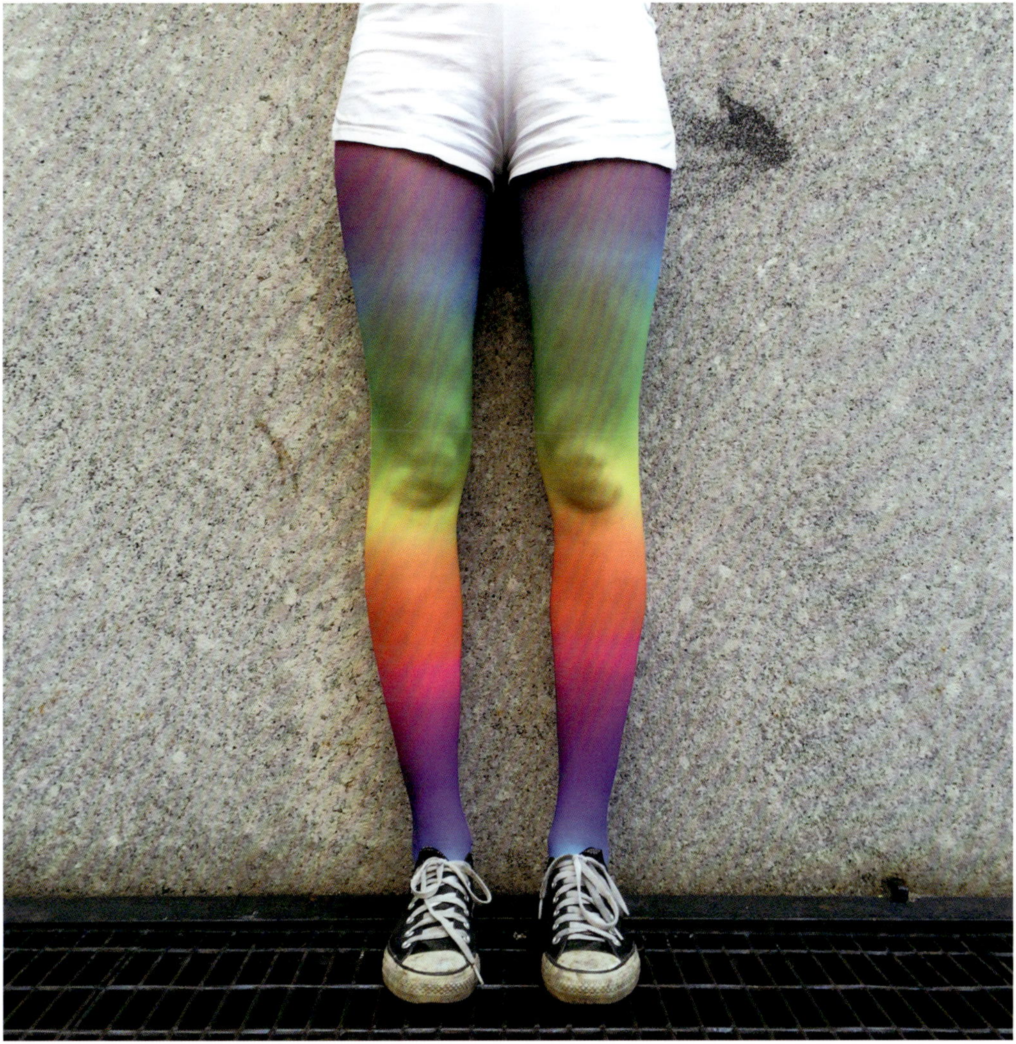

40th St., between 7th & 8th Aves.

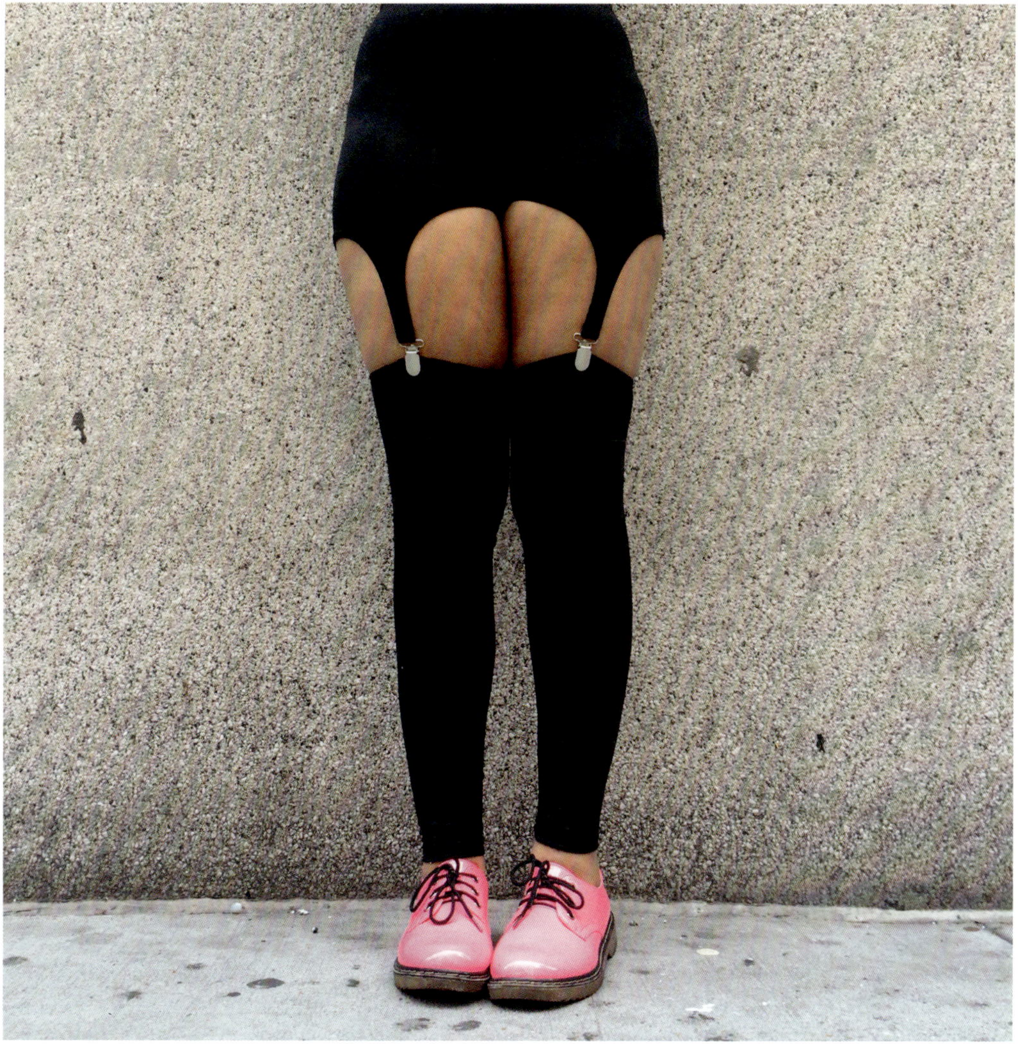

125th St. & Saint Nicholas Ave.

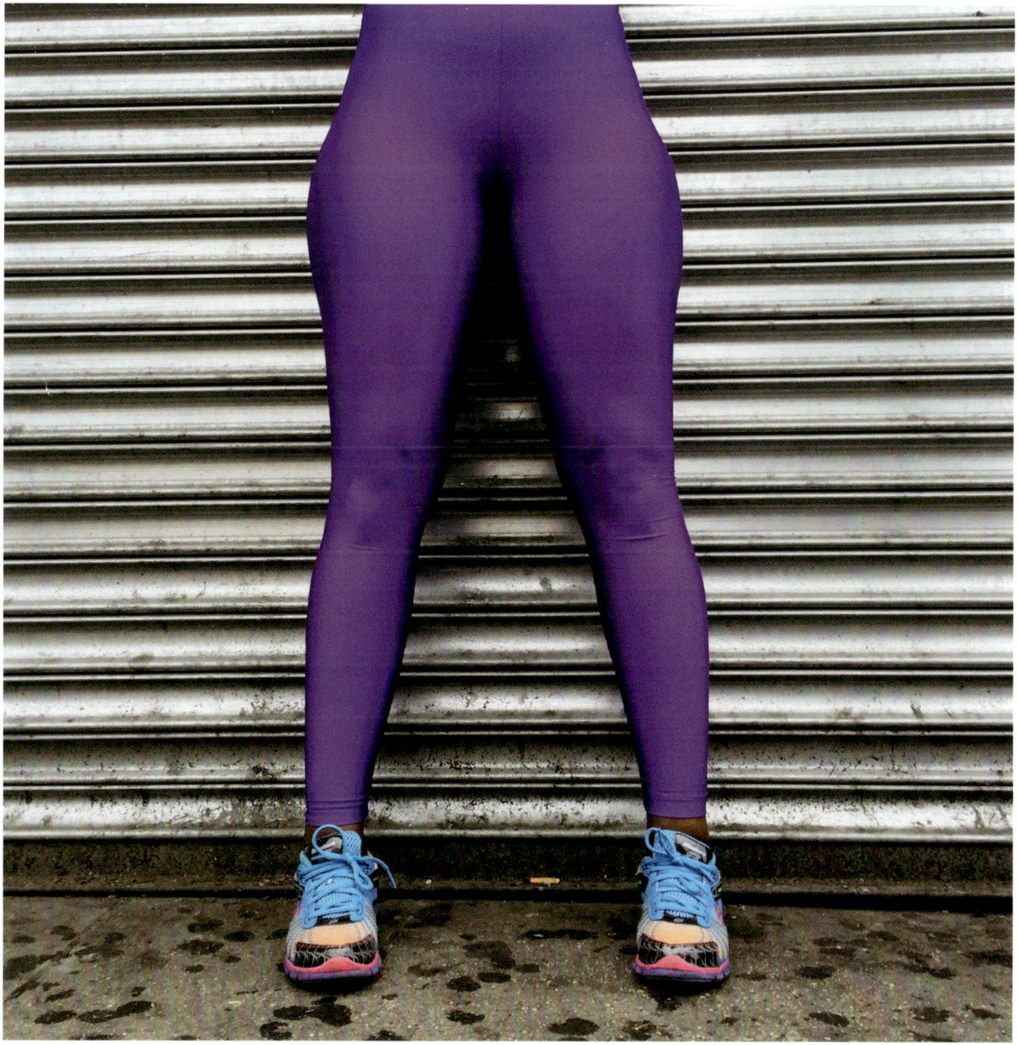

48th St., near Park Ave.

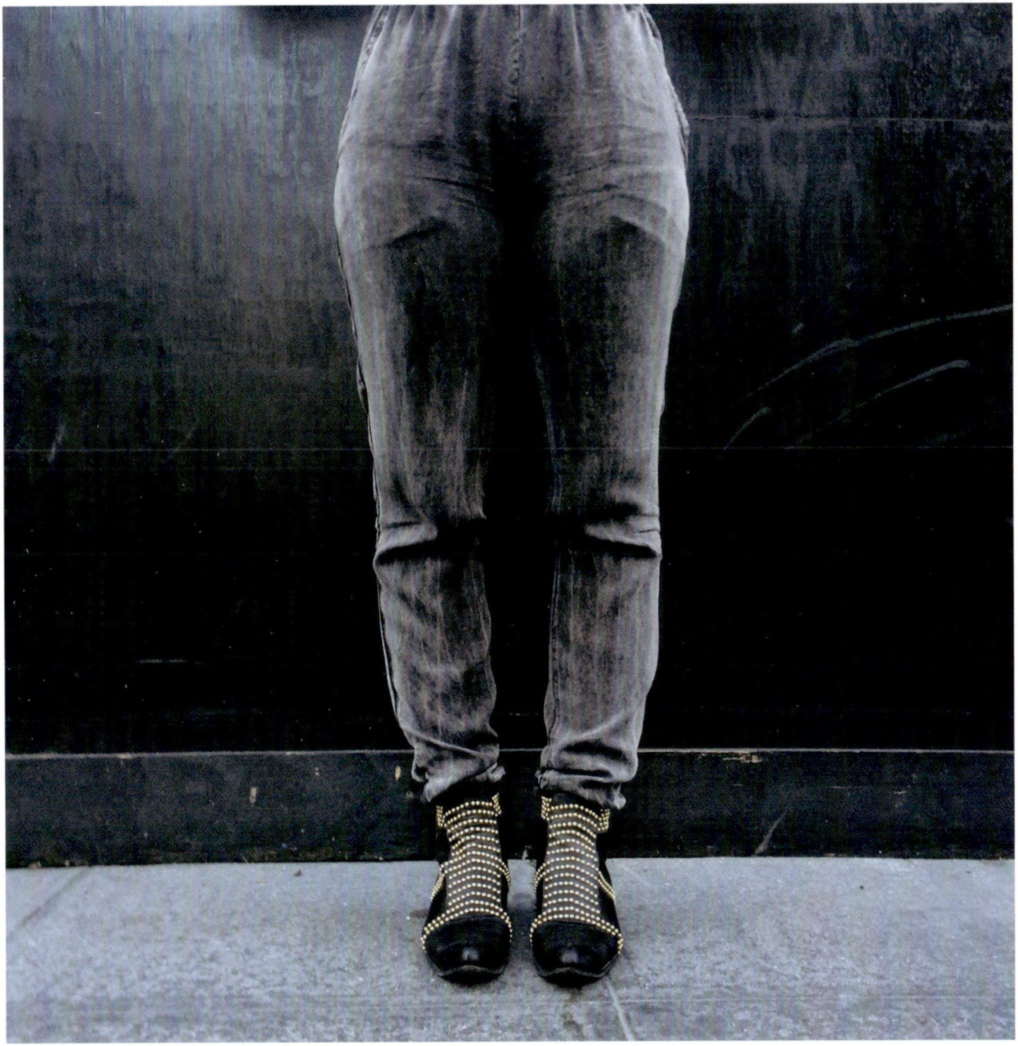

56th St. & 8th Ave.

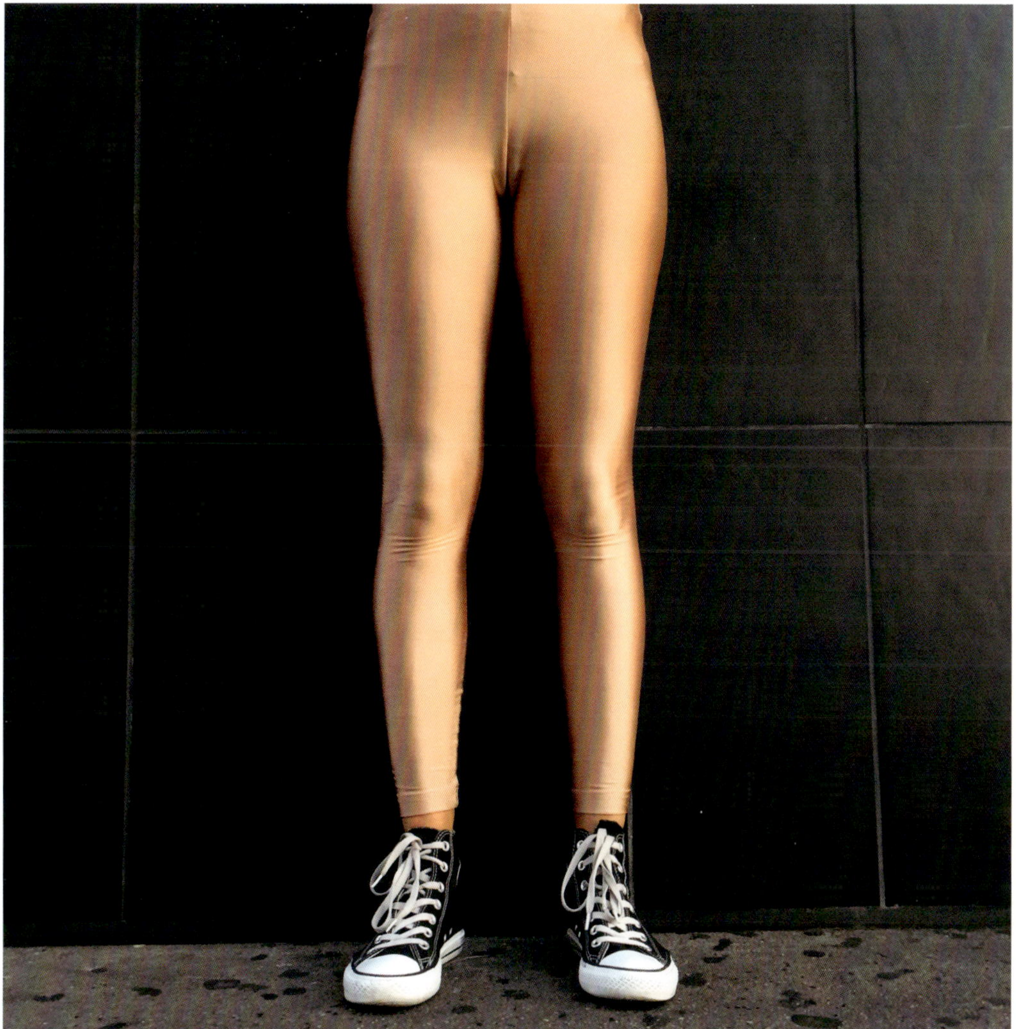

Park Ave., near 125th St.

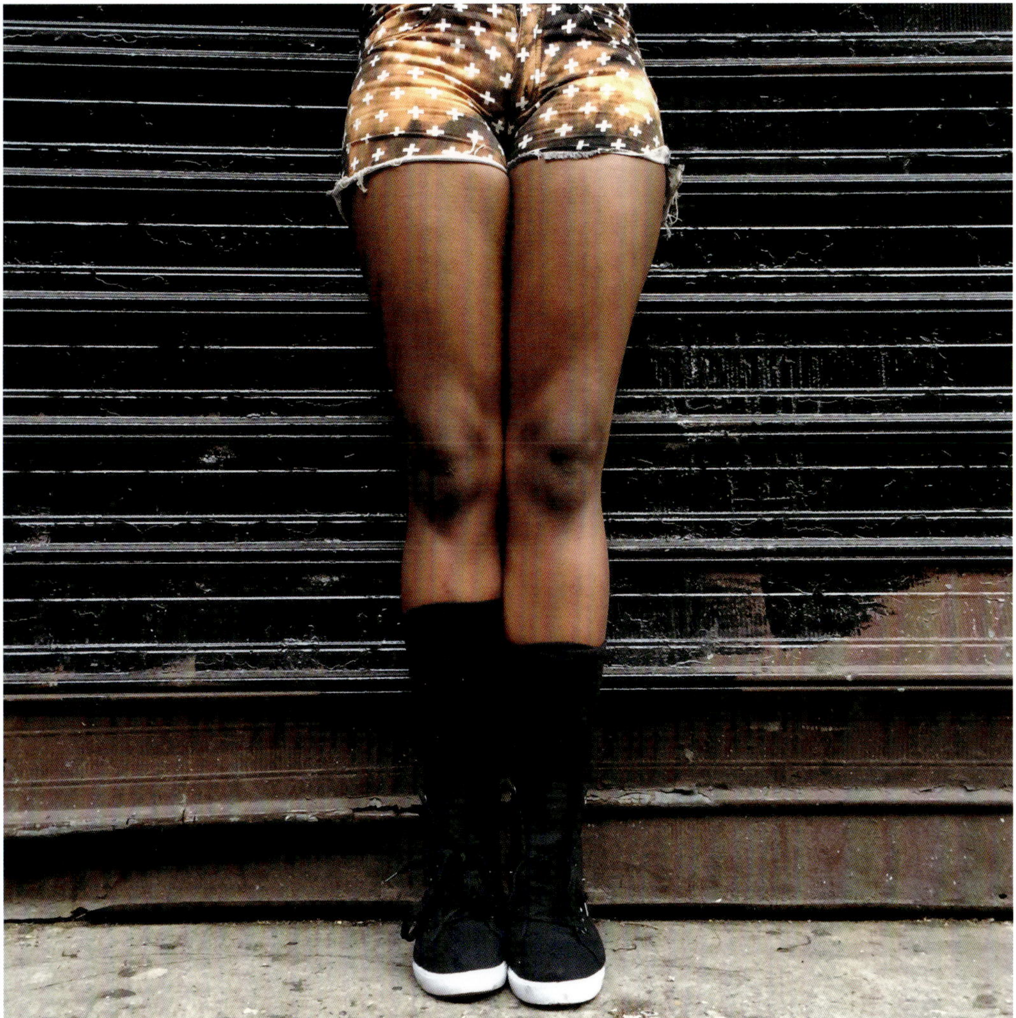

40th St., between 7th & 8th Aves.

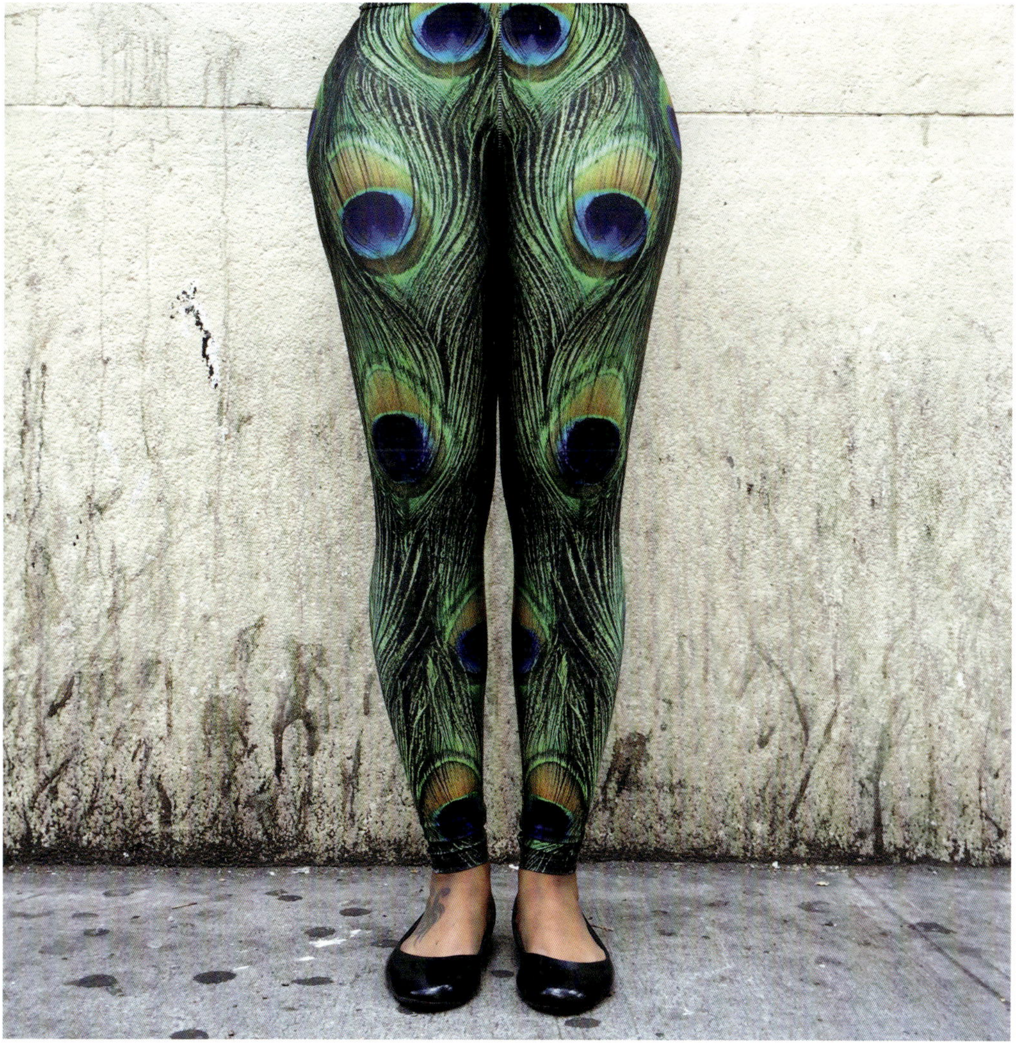

Saint Nicholas Ave. & 125th St.

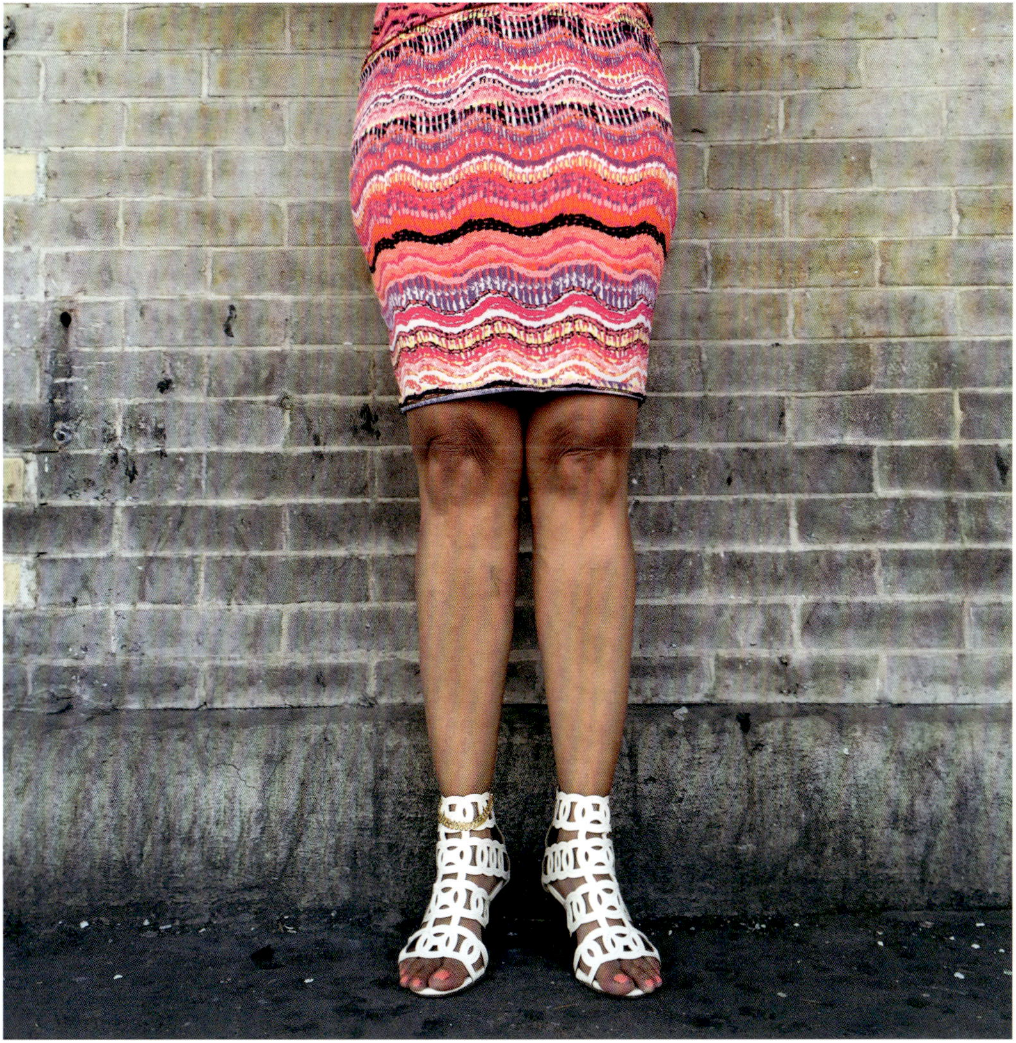

125th St., near Malcolm X Blvd.

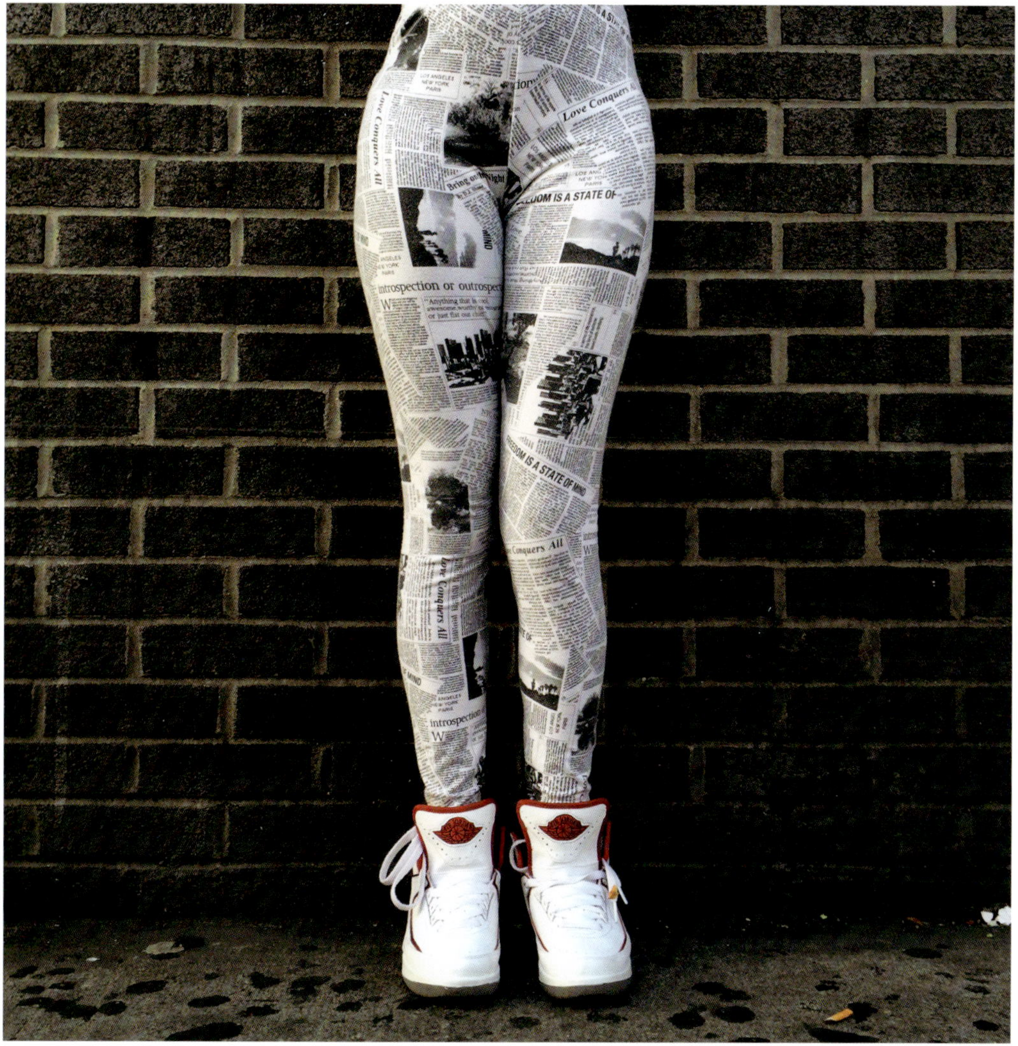
Love Conquers All
FREEDOM IS A STATE OF MIND
LOS ANGELES
NEW YORK
PARIS

75th St. & Madison Ave.

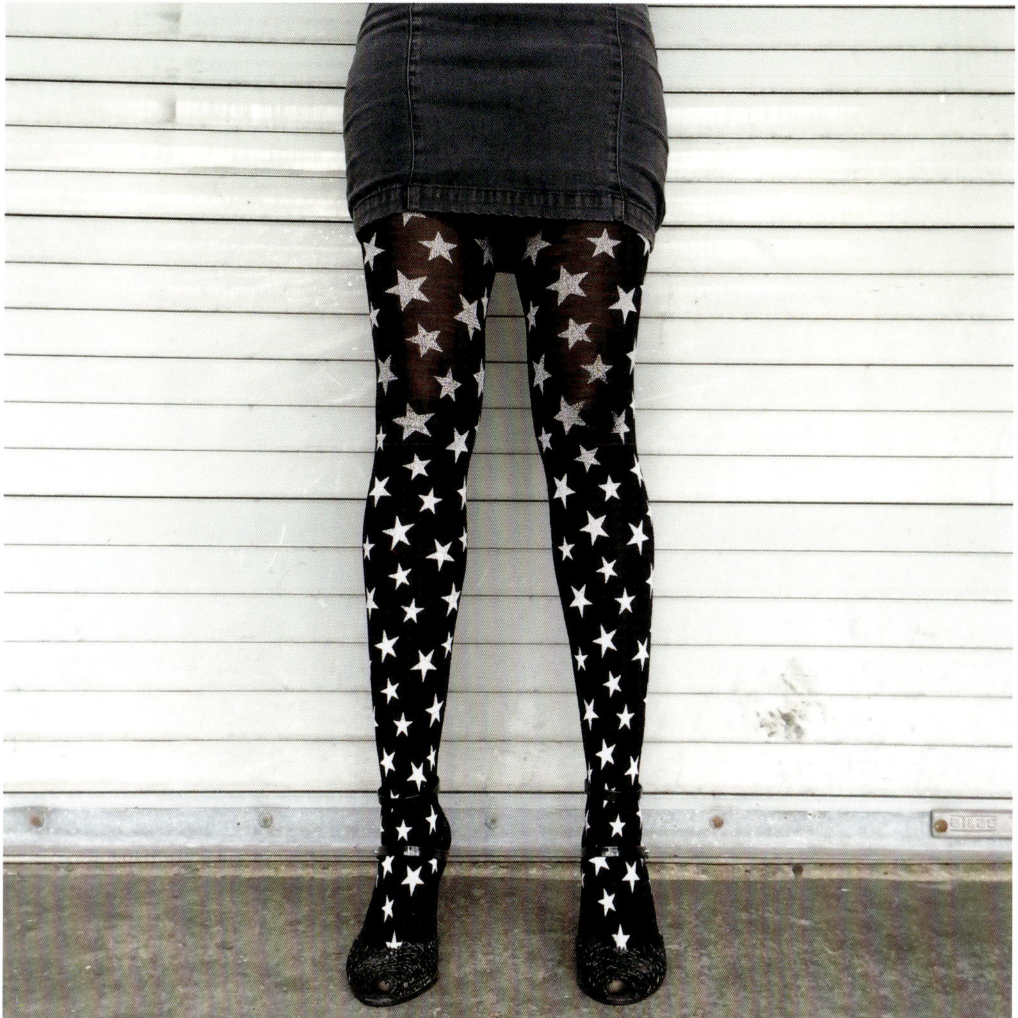

51st St. & 8th Ave.

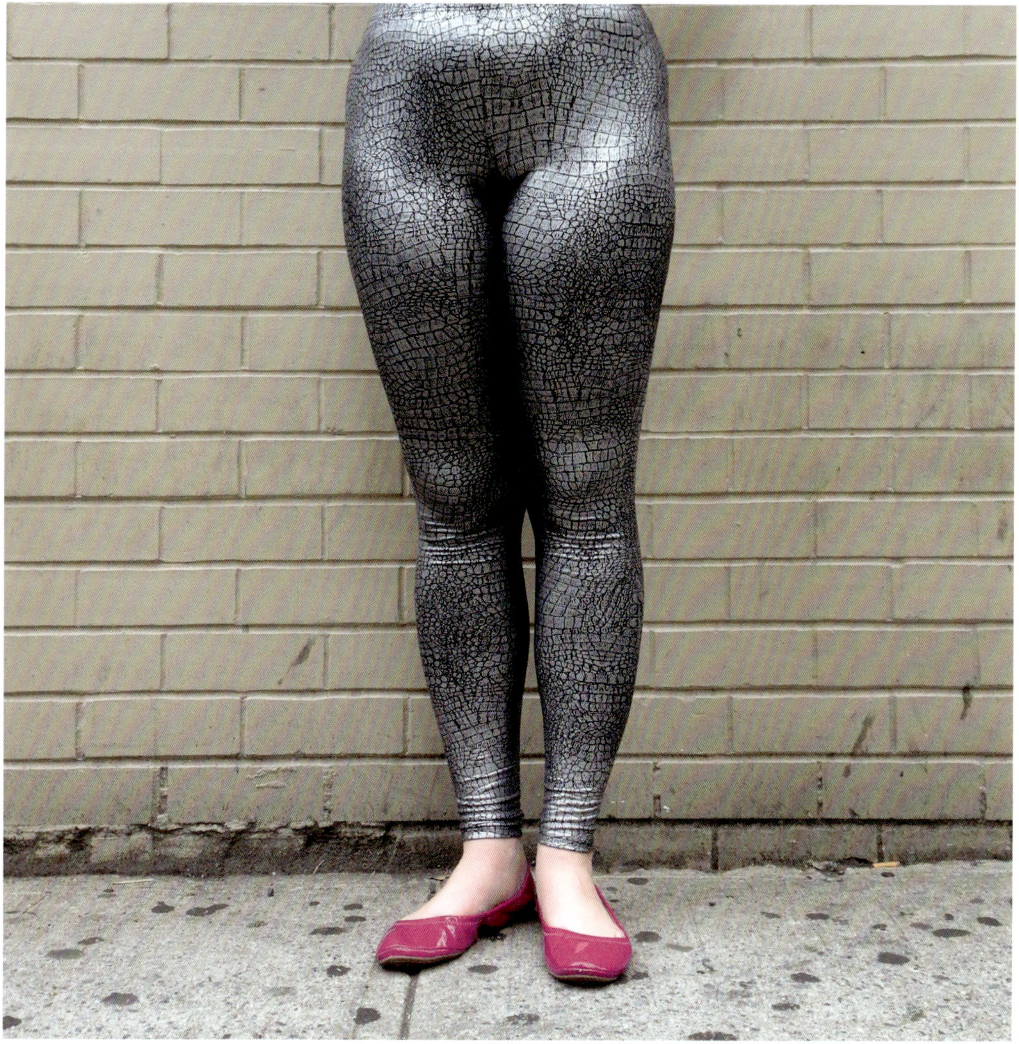

40th St., between 7th & 8th Aves.

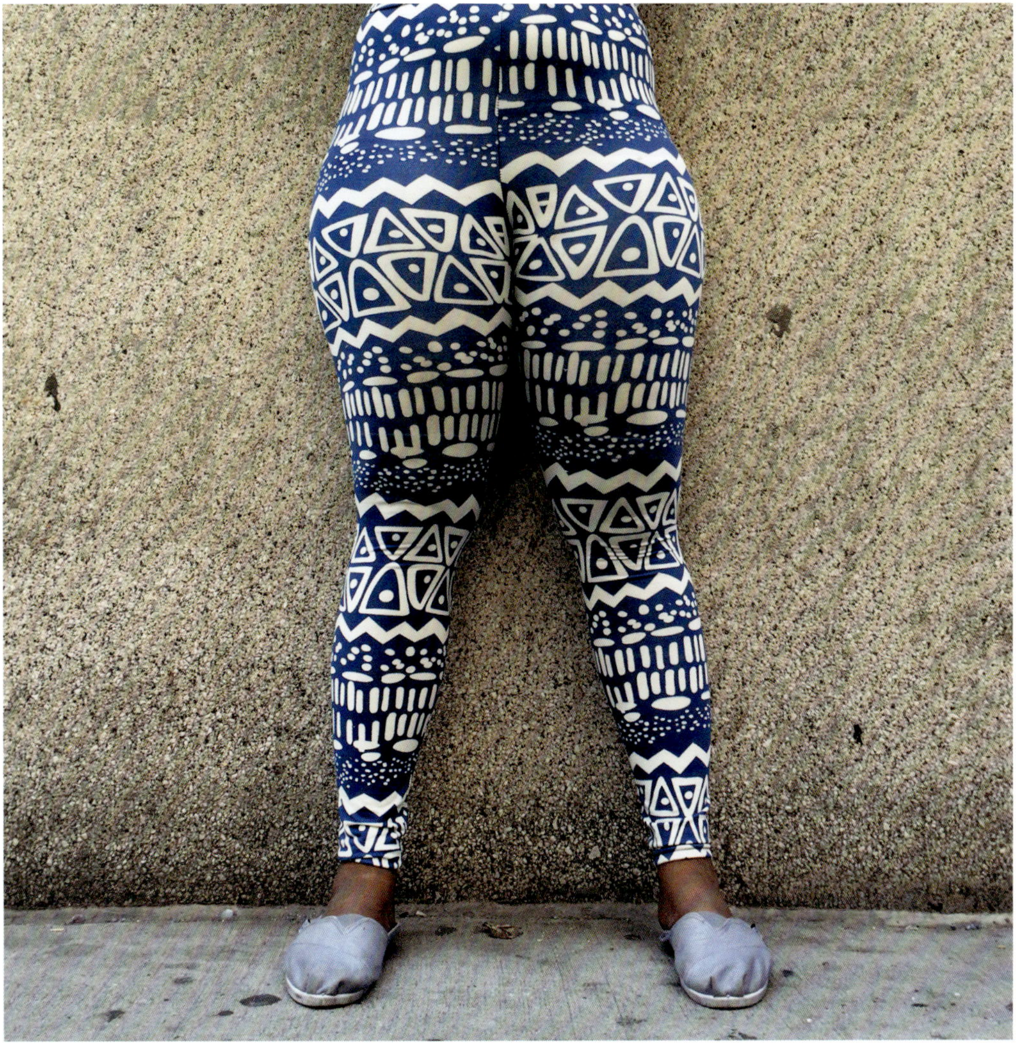

86th St., between 3rd & Lexington Aves.

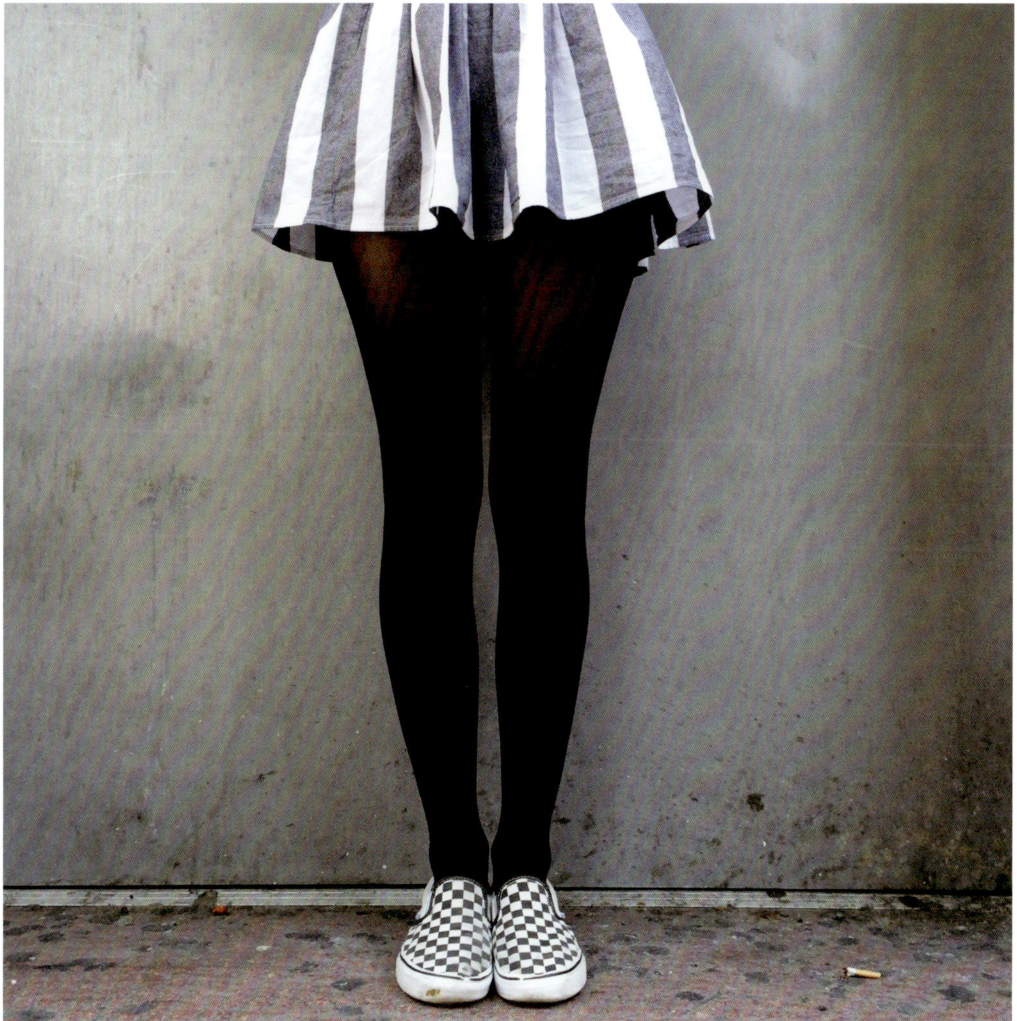

52nd St. & 8th Ave.

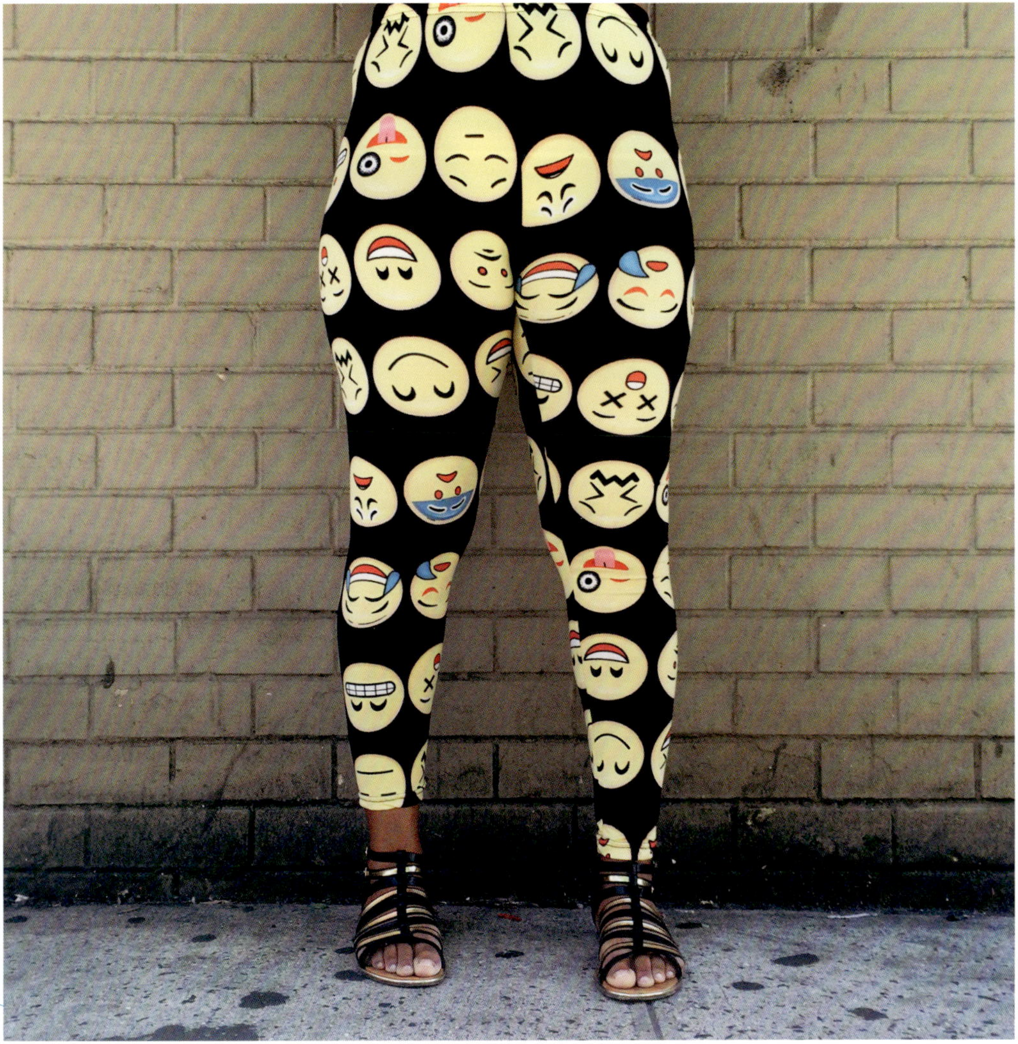

53rd St. & 8th Ave.

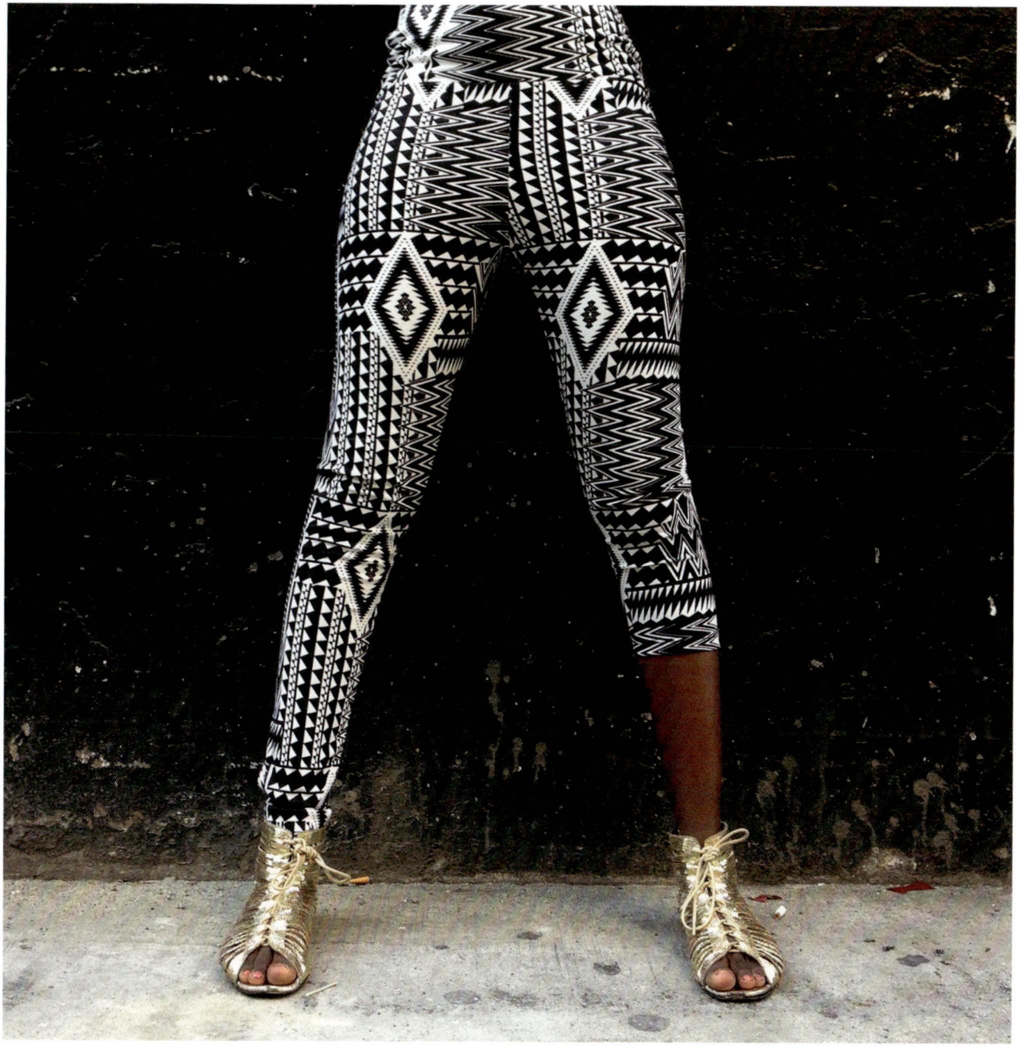

Thank you to all of the women who stopped and allowed this stranger to take their photographs.

And to Markus Hartmann, Art Streiber, Jason Polan, Noel Bowler, Hans Seeger, Yvette Monahan, B.J. Jacobs, Kenneth O Halloran, David Vecsey, Carrie Thompson, Ethan Jones, Harvey Dickson, Karen Hanley, Cybele Grandjean, Alec Soth, Jim Casper, Galen Fletcher, Scott Thode, Drea Zlanabitnig, Walter Green, Caleb Bennett, Ben Grandgenett, Gabrielle Plucknette, Marvin Orellana, Yuko and my parents.

And especially to Matt Willey and Kathy Ryan.